"Outstanding and timely. This book allows people to enrich their personal lives through the use of practical, workable, everyday methods."

Peggy Bassett, D.D.
President, United Church of Religious Science

"I highly recommend this comprehensive and valuable book to all those who are seeking a deeper understanding of themselves and who wish to change their responses to the people in their lives."

Rev. Jack Boland
Unity Church of Today.
Warren, MI

"A unique and important adjunct to therapy. Helps people focus quickly and deeply on their issues while providing a practical process for continuing their learning. This book forms a valuable part of the support system that people need to make meaningful changes."

Jilla Wolsey
Past President
California Association of Marriage & Family Therapists

"The warmth and sensitivity expressed in the Paul's earlier books is equalled only by the usability of *From Conflict to Caring*. The book lends itself to becoming an integral part of the structure of outpatient therapy."

Barbara Burns
Director, Educational Services
Growth Associates Prairie View Inc.
Wichita, KS

"An extremely valuable guide to finally express the caring and loving nature that we all truly possess."

Rev. Tifanie Blossom
Church of Religious Science
Toledo, OH

From Conflict to Caring

to

Caring

An In-depth Program for
Creating Loving Relationships

Drs. Jordan & Margaret Paul

CompCare®
Publishers

2415 Annapolis Lane
Minneapolis, Minnesota 55441

The following have generously given permission to use quotations from
copyrighted works: "Principles for Relationships" adapted from "Couples Course
Principles" by Robert and Judith Shaw of the Family Institute of Berkeley,
California. Reprinted by permission of the authors. "Do You Act — or React?" by
Sidney J. Harris. Copyright 1989 North America Syndicate, Inc. Reprinted with
special permission of NAS, Inc. From *The Way of Transformation* by Karlfried
Gräf von Durckheim. Reprinted by permission of the publishers, Unwin Hyman
Limited.

Library of Congress Cataloging-in-Publication Data

Paul, Jordan.
From conflict to caring

   Bibliography: p.
   1. Interpersonal relations. 2. Interpersonal conflict. 3. Interpersonal
communication. 4. Love.
I. Paul, Margaret. II. Title.
HM132.P3693 1989   302.3'4   89-598
ISBN 0-89638-158-7

Cover design by Susan Rinek

All inquiries and requests to reprint should be addressed to:

CompCare Publishers
2415 Annapolis Lane
Minneapolis, MN 55441
Call toll free 800/328-3330
(Minnesota residents 612/559-4800)

  6   5   4   3   2   1
94 93 92 91 90 89

CONTENTS

ACKNOWLEDGMENTS

Thanks to all Intention Training graduates—

Your willingness to participate in the workshops gave us the opportunity to develop these exercises.

A special thanks to Jackie Benster, whose tireless efforts, intense dedication, and creative ideas were an integral part of shaping this book.

INTRODUCTION TO SECTION I

For the last twenty-five years, we have been learning and developing ideas about how relationships work, crystallizing these thoughts into models to understanding the paths through conflicts in relationships, and finally sharing with you what we've learned.

There are two primary reasons we decided to write this workbook. First, for the many people who have communicated with us asking for more help in implementing the ideas we presented in *Do I Have to Give Up Me to Be Loved By You?* and *If You Really Loved Me. . . .* In addition, this workbook contains some of the information and exercises we developed for the Intention Training Workshop. In these workshops, the learning is facilitated by group interactions, guided imagery with music, and demonstrations. The workshop—a joyous experience for us to teach—adds different dimensions to the learning experience. If you cannot join us in a workshop, we suggest you use this book, as it offers the tools for you to re-create an ongoing, in-depth learning process.

The second reason for this book is to update our readers regarding our learning over the past six years. Although our basic theory has remained intact, our learning has deepened, and with it we have developed better and better suggestions for helping other people learn in their relationships.

Throughout our life together, our most profound learning has come about as a result of our conflicts with each other. What we have learned, we have taken into other relationships—with children, parents, friends, ex-mates, clients, siblings, employees—and as a result, we have improved these relationships. In the past six years, we have become increasingly aware of the tremendous value of learning from each of the relationships in our lives.

Whenever you have conflict with anyone, you can learn from your reactions to it. Our children have given us wonderful opportunities to practice this. It is quite a challenge to respond in ways that leave us feeling best about ourselves when they behave in ways that frighten us and/or go against the values we believe to be "right." (This, of course, goes hand in hand with behaving in ways that are best for them as well.) Our relationships with our parents and grandparents also give us wonderful opportunities to practice loving behavior. Our patterned ways of behaving with them go back to the roots of our decisions about how to behave. Learning how to be loving with them often means challenging very deeply ingrained habits and beliefs.

We also have recognized the importance of learning and changing our ways in other relationships and have realized that in fact our feelings about ourselves are affected by how we relate to *everyone*. For example, although it's easy to use the power of being a boss to control employees, it's only because of our commitment to behaving in caring ways that we have the opportunity to confront our fears of letting go and being taken advantage of or being perceived as weak. Since being taken advantage of is certainly not loving to ourselves, we must learn to bring our behavior into line with the principles of love. Our relationship with Jackie, our office manager and assistant, has been a wonderful opportunity to practice these principles. We all use the relationship for our personal development, and we all have the freedom to confront one another with anything that we see or feel about our relationship.

Friends are another important part of our lives. Our best friendships are those in which everyone is willing to be honest with one another. We value people who are willing to confront us when they feel unloved by our behavior, for that is the way we can continue to grow, learn, and become even better friends. We have learned that when people surround themselves with those who are intimidated by them, or when people eliminate from their lives anyone who begins to threaten their personal power, they cut off one of the best sources of feedback for personal growth.

As therapists, we have learned much from our clients' reactions to us. For example, if clients are defensive or resistant, rather than make them wrong for their reactions and focus only on helping them to change, we also try to see our part in their reactions.

The book is divided into two sections. Section I will bring you up to date with our ideas. Section II contains practical exercises to increase your personal awareness and create change in your life.

A more complete expression of our ideas is presented in *Do I Have to Give Up Me to Be Loved by You?* and *If You Really Loved Me. . . .* We hope you will read those books, too, for they contain more in-depth information to help you along your path to growth.

Jordan and Margaret Paul
West Los Angeles

PRINCIPLES FOR RELATIONSHIPS

1. *My relationships are my opportunity to express myself as a loving person. How I express my love is a function of my own willingness to do so, not the result of how another person behaves.*

2. *Any difficult or painful moment in my relationships is a new opportunity for me to develop as a loving person. At the moment of conflict, I can choose to blame the other and the relationship, or, by my willingness to learn from the experience, I can use the occasion to expand my ability to love and to learn.*

3. *I am the one who generates my experience of my relationships through how I choose to act and react to whatever anyone does, and I am solely responsible for my feelings.*

4. *All my life's partners (mate, children, parents, friends) love me in their Higher Selves as I love them in my Higher Self.* * *My partners are lovable in their Higher Selves as I am lovable in my Higher Self.*

5. *I can experience love and satisfaction whenever I choose. These feelings are possible at any time and place and in any circumstance, whenever I choose to be who I really am, my Higher Self.*

*A note to all readers: We use *Higher Self* as Twelve Step groups use the term *Higher Power:* To allow individuals to approach God, or the God within them, with their own personal meaning.

· 1 ·

FROM CONFLICT TO CARING

LOVING BEHAVIOR

In *Do I Have to Give Up Me to Be Loved by You?*, when we first developed our model of the paths through conflict, we understood that the closed, defensive, protected path necessarily leads to negative consequences. We also knew that the open, vulnerable, learning path leads to positive consequences. And we knew that all of us can choose which path to take.

For example, let's say that your mate forgets your birthday and you feel upset. You can protect yourself by blaming your partner, who may then get angry, which hurts you, and then you both retreat, feeling unloved and unloving. Or you can gently remind your mate, openly ask why he/she forgot your birthday, explore your reactions (why you've taken it personally, what your expectations are, and how you react when your expectations aren't met), and experience the entirely different result of acting from an intention to learn. Clearly, the choice of the reaction is yours. And as you make your choice, *the things you do generate the feelings you feel*.

The most important addition to this understanding of the paths through conflict emerged when we discovered, in *The Road Less Traveled,* by M. Scott Peck, the following definition: ''[Loving behavior is] the will to extend one's self for the purpose of nurturing one's own or another's spiritual growth.'' This sparked thoughts that added a much deeper dimension to our thinking—the dimension of love and caring and the recognition of the difference between loving feelings and loving behavior. (We will use the words *loving* and *caring* interchangeably.)

First, for most people, there is a big difference between the love they say they feel and what their behavior indicates. All too often when conflict occurs, people who say they love each other do not act out the love they feel; instead, they act out their protections.

Second, while on one hand the things you do generate your feelings, on the other hand *your feelings generate the things you do*. So, if on a deep level you love someone but your behavior isn't loving, there must be another feeling getting in the way. Almost every time, that intervening feeling is some form of fear, guilt, or shame. As we said in *Do I Have to Give Up Me to Be Loved by You?*, the opposite of love is not hate, it is fear.

The next conclusion became obvious: the intention to learn, which we had labeled the "path of evolution," is the path not only of growth but, more important, of loving behavior. And the opposite—the path of fear and protection—is unloving behavior.

We have therefore expanded our definition as follows: Loving behavior nurtures your own and another's emotional and spiritual growth, promotes personal responsibility, and increases self-esteem.

Our model illustrates the only two intentions possible in a conflict—the intention to learn or the intention to protect—and the paths that follow each intent. Conflict—any situation that produces discomfort, feelings of fear, guilt, anger, disappointment, or hurt—occurs when another person does something you don't like or think is wrong, or when *you* do something that another person doesn't like or thinks is wrong; or you do something *you* think is wrong, which creates internal conflict. The instantaneous, learned reaction to conflict is to protect. You choose it, albeit subconsciously, because the conflict taps in to many fears, and you believe that reacting openly would leave you too vulnerable. These deeply ingrained beliefs and fears, which were learned in childhood and lie buried in your subconscious, have been causing you to react protectively to internal and external conflicts since you were an infant; these responses, which have become habit, have produced the patterned reactions that run your life.

In addition, we've all learned to respond protectively to *any* discomfort, not just the discomfort produced by conflict. We've learned to protect against feelings of anxiety, disappointment, sadness, grief, guilt, disconnection, aloneness, boredom, hurt, and fear. And just as there are only two intentions in a conflict, there are only two intentions in response to any discomfort—protecting against feeling, trying to make feelings go away by denying them, or feeling our feelings so that we can learn about the fears and beliefs that are creating our discomfort.

There are three categories of protective reactions: (1) control—attempting to get others to change their behavior through instilling fear or guilt; (2) compliance—going along with what others want, out of fear or guilt; (3) noncompliance—either active resistance, which is rebelling; passive resistance, which is temporary compliance followed by deferred resistance (you say you will but then you don't); or indifference, which is either withdrawing or shutting out, or both. None of the things you do to protect yourself—those behaviors that cover up your vulnerable feelings of hurt and fear—meet the definition of loving behavior.

In both our personal and professional lives, we were aware of our protective behaviors. It was relatively simple to see that our attempts to control people or to give ourselves up were not leading to intimacy. But to realize that these behaviors were unloving hit us like a ton of bricks.

It's easy to be loving when things go your way, but when people do things you don't like, your subconscious fears rise closer to the surface, causing you to react habitually with protective, unloving behavior, which inevitably results in the other person's getting upset and behaving unloving toward you. Then either you give in, hoping to placate the other person and regain his/her love, or you become rebellious or walled off behind your indifference, or you attempt to get the other to change his/her unloving behavior. Of course, the other person then reacts to your defenses with his/her own defenses—and a protective circle is created.

Understanding loving behavior made it disturbingly evident that *unhappiness is always a direct result of unloving behavior*. The most challenging path you can pursue is learning to react in a caring way to yourself and another person *no matter what the other person is doing.*

To see compliant behavior as unloving is a real stretch for most people. After all, you have been taught that giving in, going along with, and/or pleasing others at your own expense is loving. But seeing that none of these behaviors fosters your own or others' emotional and spiritual growth casts an entirely different light on your behavior.

Unloving behavior starts the erosion process that leads to alienation and unhappiness. The unspoken message you give over and over again to the people in your life is, "I'll be caring with you as long as you behave the way I think you should."

Protective, unloving behaviors not only estrange you from the people in your life but cause unhappiness within you. Protective behavior does not nurture your emotional and spiritual growth and is not personally responsible. Consequently, protective, unloving behavior diminishes your self-esteem.

The corollary insight is just as important and may be more surprising: your self-esteem is raised or lowered by how you react to conflict. Protective responses—attempting to control, giving in, becoming indifferent—lower self-esteem. You feel weak, out of control, like a victim. Conversely, loving behavior, an openness to learning, feels powerful: you are in control of yourself; you are not a reactor but are taking positive action.

Protections—your attempts to avoid the pain of losing either another person's love or your own integrity—actually bring about the very things you hope to avoid: lowered self-esteem; eroding love; power struggles; sexual, financial, and communication squabbles; feeling unloved and unloving.

Protective, unloving circles continue to bring about the misery in your life. Anytime you see another person's behavior as wrong and try to get him/her to change, or you go along with it out of guilt or fear, or you become indifferent, you perpetuate an unloving circle.

The intention to learn, however, fits the definition of loving behavior and produces entirely different results—personally responsible behavior, emotional and spiritual growth, and joy, intimacy, satisfaction, and self-esteem. Anything other than an intention to learn is protective.

When you're open to learning from conflict you want to understand yourself and the other person. You want to learn from your feelings rather than protect against them. The intention to learn begins a process of exploration that requires only two conditions: (1) a willingness to experience the transitory pain that may accompany the truth; and (2) a belief that there are very important, compelling, respectable reasons behind every behavior and feeling. The areas that can be explored are: how you protect; what happens when you protect; what are the fears and beliefs that produce your protections; how you got these fears and beliefs and the purpose they now serve; and what it means to take personal responsibility and to be loving.

When we wrote *Do I Have to Give Up Me to Be Loved by You?* our primary focus was on exploring and learning about the other person. We have learned, however, that the primary focus must be on learning about *oneself*. Learning about the other is important, but focusing on oneself is the key to being personally responsible. In fact, focusing on the other can be just another way to protect oneself from looking inward and taking responsibility.

One of the questions we are most often asked is, "How can I practice these ideas if the person I'm in conflict with is not open to exploring and learning?" When your intention is to learn about yourself, the other person is merely your helper. You can do your learning with or without him/her. In a primary love relationship, the involvement of your mate creates a wonderful intimacy; but if you believe you can't learn without the involvement of that person, you become a victim, anxiously awaiting your partner's decision to be open or not. However, you do not need to wait for another's cooperation. You become a victim only by choice. When the other person is not available, you can learn about yourself by looking at your part in creating the conflict, or you can read, think, write, or enlist the help of a friend or therapist.

We all want love, and we wait for others to give it to us, but love and good feelings occur in our lives only as we become more loving. The charge becomes obvious: you need to stop trying to get others to change and concentrate on what you need to do to become more loving.

Our up-to-date revised chart follows, illustrating the paths through conflict.

THE PATHS THROUGH CONFLICT

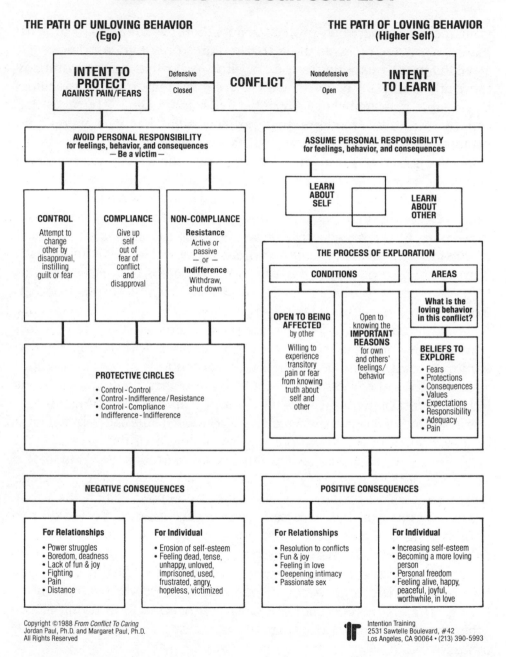

THE PATH OF UNLOVING BEHAVIOR
(Ego)

THE PATH OF LOVING BEHAVIOR
(Higher Self)

INTENT TO PROTECT
AGAINST PAIN/FEARS

Defensive
Closed

CONFLICT

Nondefensive
Open

INTENT TO LEARN

AVOID PERSONAL RESPONSIBILITY
for feelings, behavior, and consequences
— Be a victim —

ASSUME PERSONAL RESPONSIBILITY
for feelings, behavior, and consequences

LEARN ABOUT SELF

LEARN ABOUT OTHER

CONTROL

Attempt to change other by disapproval, instilling guilt or fear

COMPLIANCE

Give up self out of fear of conflict and disapproval

NON-COMPLIANCE

Resistance
Active or passive
— or —
Indifference
Withdraw, shut down

THE PROCESS OF EXPLORATION

CONDITIONS

AREAS

OPEN TO BEING AFFECTED
by other

Willing to experience transitory pain or fear from knowing truth about self and other

Open to knowing the **IMPORTANT REASONS** for own and others' feelings/ behavior

What is the loving behavior in this conflict?

BELIEFS TO EXPLORE
• Fears
• Protections
• Consequences
• Values
• Expectations
• Responsibility
• Adequacy
• Pain

PROTECTIVE CIRCLES
• Control - Control
• Control - Indifference / Resistance
• Control - Compliance
• Indifference - Indifference

NEGATIVE CONSEQUENCES

POSITIVE CONSEQUENCES

For Relationships
• Power struggles
• Boredom, deadness
• Lack of fun & joy
• Fighting
• Pain
• Distance

For Individual
• Erosion of self-esteem
• Feeling dead, tense, unhappy, unloved, imprisoned, used, frustrated, angry, hopeless, victimized

For Relationships
• Resolution to conflicts
• Fun & joy
• Feeling in love
• Deepening intimacy
• Passionate sex

For Individual
• Increasing self-esteem
• Becoming a more loving person
• Personal freedom
• Feeling alive, happy, peaceful, joyful, worthwhile, in love

Intention Training
2531 Sawtelle Boulevard, #42
Los Angeles, CA 90064 • (213) 390-5993

The intention to learn in conflict occurs rarely. Yet it is the only way you can learn the way out of your unhappiness and into love. Any situation that upsets you—unmet expectations, disappointments, broken commitments, and so on—provides an opportuntiy for your most profound learning. Such situations can be met with either the intention to protect or the intention to learn. When you react protectively, you do not learn anything. When you are open to learning, you create meaningful changes in your life.

In every conflict, the question never asked is, "What is the loving behavior?" Because you haven't been trained to think in these terms, you need first to learn what is loving and then to learn what prevents you from behaving that way. An openness to learning is always loving. Reacting in protective, unloving ways will guarantee negative results. It's the same set of interactions that guarantees war between nations: we get upset, believe we're right ("God is on our side!"), and go to war; or we defend ourselves from a real or imagined threat by going to war. Even though at times fighting may be necessary to survive, the belief that we can bring about peace by going to war is a false belief. Real peace will only emerge from a total change in consciousness. Learning what it means to relate to others with love *is* that consciousness.

The history of our culture shows a distressing picture of an unloving people. Ego consciousness—judgmentalness, self-righteousness, dominance, one-upmanship, selfishness, accumulation of power—has been predominant. But we are now at a unique crossroads: either we learn to live in peace or we will destroy our planet. Only when we become convinced that our old ways of thinking will never bring about peace and joy will we be ready to behave from the consciousness of love. And the beginning of that consciousness is learning to relate lovingly to each other in our everyday lives.

Relationship, then, is the new frontier and we all are the pioneers. It's both frightening and exciting. There are not many models to help us learn how to play this new game. Most books about relationships reflect old ways of thinking. Everyone is struggling to discover what it means to have truly loving relationships, but no one has all the answers. However, we can unlock our potential to live more closely with the part of ourselves that has long been dormant— our Higher Selves, the consciousness of love that lies within us all. As we live more in harmony with that consciousness, we will open vast new possibilities.

SELF-LIMITING BELIEFS

Removing the blocks to being a more loving person has become the focus of our personal learning and teaching. Protection—the exact opposite of loving behavior, which is to be open, giving (without giving up oneself), soft, and concerned for self and others—is always a reaction to fear. *The real basis of fear, guilt, and shame is false beliefs.* In fact, all negative feelings come from false beliefs. So, when you change your beliefs, your feelings will change.

Beliefs run your life, and most of your beliefs are erroneous and self-limiting. For example, when you believe you're inadequate in a particular area (how your body looks, your intelligence, your sensitivity), you take things personally and feel bad and defensive when you're criticized. Your feelings come directly from your belief of inadequacy. When you know you're okay, even though criticism never feels good, you clearly see that the criticism comes from the other person's false beliefs and his/her own unhealed pain, and your feelings and reactions are entirely different.

You may not fully understand how your beliefs create the fears that generate your behavior. In fact, you may not believe it at all. However, it's true, and we'll be coming back to it over and over again. Throughout this book are lists of self-limiting beliefs, designed to help you discover how many self-limiting beliefs you have. When you decide to rid yourself of false beliefs, you'll begin to live more consistently with the truth.

AN EMOTIONAL, INTELLECTUAL, PHILOSOPHICAL, AND SPIRITUAL JOURNEY

You were not born with beliefs about right or wrong. Rather, from conception on, you were guided by an unseen intelligence that knew exactly how to behave and feel. You didn't think, you just reacted. The beliefs you later used to guide your life were learned. The truth you now seek in the learning process comes from the part of yourself that we refer to as the Higher Self. The Higher Self has been called by many names—the Holy Spirit, Christ consciousness, natural self, human nature, God. Use whatever words feel most comfortable for you.

This Higher Self is an extension of the energy that created and maintains everything. It is the part of you that knows how to live in a loving and joyful way. The intention to learn is a journey to rediscover and to live more harmoniously with that part of yourself.

The Higher Self state of being is not well known. The personality you formed soon after birth is the more familiar. This learned persona is your ego.

We use the word *ego* as it is used in Eastern philosophy— meaning the constructed personality, the false self. The definition of *ego* in Western thinking has come from Freudian psychology. By that definition, the ego is the governor of the personality structure that includes the ego, the superego, and the id, and therefore a strong ego is considered a healthy thing. But when defined as the false self, a dominant ego is not desirable.

As you grew up, your constructed personality or ego was an important part of your development and became your defense system. You came into the world defenseless, guided mostly by instinct, your natural self. Your behavior, however, was judged by just about everyone, and was reacted to with anything from a disapproving look to yelling, spanking, or enforced isolation. But the message was clear: "You are wrong." You were made wrong for your thoughts, feelings, and actions, and were judged as bad every time your behavior conflicted with what those around you believed was right. Into your ego went all of the beliefs you learned.

The ego was created, then, to protect you when your natural actions and feelings brought disapproval from those around you. As a child, the fear of rejection was so great that you had to create a way to avoid this disapproval and gain the love you so desperately needed. Your ego was necessary; it saved your sanity, if not your life.

15

The ego, born out of fear, does not know how to love. It is the needy part of you that only wants to get, to manipulate others to give you love, affirmation, and approval. All fears of inadequacy and the beliefs that created those fears are in your ego.

For most of us, our personalities become so identified with our egos that we forget we have another part of our being—the Higher Self. It is the part of you that is connected to, and in harmony with, the universe. It functions from universal truths rather than from the beliefs of human beings. It is the best that is within you. In the Higher Self there are no judgments, fears, worries, or protections, for it is the place of unconditional love and knowingness. The Higher Self is love, and it exists in all of us and we all have access to it.

It's important to recognize times when you've been in harmony with that part of you and recognize the feelings that always accompany Higher Self behavior. (We have included an exercise to help you do that on page 81.) It is that centered, balanced, wholesome place where you act with integrity and feel your self-esteem enhanced. When your behavior comes from the Higher Self, you feel like you're walking on water, as opposed to being stuck in the quagmire of your ego's emotions.

THE EGO VERSUS THE HIGHER SELF

All negative feelings come from the ego. The Higher Self knows only peace, love, and joy. The ego tries to justify unloving behavior—"He deserved it"; "I had to teach him a lesson"; "It was for her own good." The Higher Self never acts in an unloving way, no matter what another person is doing. In essence, that is the message taught by Buddha, Jesus, Rabbi Hillel, Gandhi, and Martin Luther King, Jr.

The Higher Self is the spiritual part of you and the only true reality. The ego is fear. The Higher Self is love. You cannot be in fear and in love at the same time—you can only be in one or the other. So in your Higher Self, free from fear, you feel alive, joyful, and relaxed.

The false beliefs of the ego tell you that you are too vulnerable and need to be protected, which forces you to act in unloving, defensive ways, creating deadness, depression, anger, and tension. The Higher Self, however, knows the truth—that you can handle, survive, and find peace in any situation.

Your ego is probably having a field day right now, pointing out all kinds of situations that you can't handle: your mate leaves you, has an affair, won't make love with you, or dies; your boss gets angry with you or you get fired; your business fails; your child fails in school or gets involved with drugs. We cannot stress strongly enough that *any* situation can be learned from and turned into a positive experience. Only when you know that any conflict or discomfort is an opportunity can you accept turmoil, chaos, and unhappiness rather than protecting against them.

All of the ego's beliefs are lies. One of the most common of these is that happiness and self-esteem come from outside yourself. Therefore, most people pursue happiness and self-esteem by trying to become successful (accomplishing things or acquiring wealth, status, or a good reputation) and/or by being loved. But the closed doors of protected thinking keep you from discovering the truth: that even if you satisfy all the ego's desires, there remains a necessary element that if not part of your life will negate everything you do.

That element is the ability to remain open and loving—in other words, in your Higher Self—when faced with difficult, upsetting situations. You have been led to believe that you will feel good about yourself when you *get* love, so most of your behavior is an attempt to get approval (or avoid disapproval) and is therefore manipulative or defensive. In reality, it's only when you *give* love that your self-esteem, your self-worth, is raised. "Giving love" means "that behavior which nurtures emotional and spiritual growth."

What the ego doesn't tell you is that the *only* way to find real happiness, peace, love and self-esteem is to behave in loving ways. Things like money and relationships can enhance your joy but can never create joy.

Protected, you get angry when things don't go your way, on your timetable, by your form. Open, you recognize that there is a higher wisdom guiding your life and that you can tap into that knowing for guidance through seemingly your darkest hours. You can wallow in the misery of self-righteous indignation, or you can learn your lesson and move on into higher self-esteem and joy. You always have two choices—to protect or to learn.

The intention to learn is a choice that you can make at any time. Our egos would like us to believe that our emotions dictate our lives so that we really don't have choice. But, as with all ego beliefs, that is false. *We always have choice.* At the Intention Training Foundation, we have a symbol that's formed by your index and middle fingers held up in a V in front of your face. The left finger represents the intention to protect, the right finger the intention to learn. The choice is always right in front of you.

You may be feeling very angry, critical, and disapproving of yourself right now. Those thoughts are coming from your ego. Try to think of yourself as a television set with only two channels. When you're critical or hard on yourself, you're tuned to your fear channel and are hearing the voice of your ego. But the other channel—your love channel—is your Higher Self. Your Higher Self, being nonjudgmental, is never critical and knows that all things have a purpose, a time, a reason. You can tune in anytime and listen to the voice of your Higher Self.

A realistic goal is to diminish the ego's control of your life. The more fear dominates you, the more unhappy you are. Conversely, the more you react in concert and in harmony with your Higher Self, the happier you are and the more love, intimacy, and joy you create.

Learning about your ego's fears and beliefs is the way out. The more you resolve your fears by bringing your beliefs into alignment with universal truths, the less time you'll spend in your ego. The task is an ongoing one. It is the challenge of a lifetime—not a week, month, or year.

THE BASIC ERROR IN OUR THINKING

The most basic, pervasive error in our thinking is that we are wrong, inadequate, unimportant, unlovable, and unworthy. Our protections surround this cavern of self-doubt and most of our unhappiness results from our attempts to protect ourselves from these feelings.

In the course of our lives, especially at the beginning, we receive thousands of messages that we're wrong. In *The Magic of Conflict*, Tom Crum quotes a study done in Iowa by graduate students following a normal two-year-old throughout a day: "They observed that the child was told what not to do 432 times, as opposed to 32 positive acknowledgments. The national average of parent-to-child criticisms is 12 to 1—that is, 12 criticisms to 1 compliment. Within the average secondary school classroom, the ratio of criticism to compliments is 18 to 1 between teacher and student." Every time an adult gets upset with a child and doesn't take responsibility for it, the adult is blaming the child and making the child wrong. A small child does not possess the wisdom to react to an older person's disapproval by thinking, "It's not that *I'm* unlovable. *You're* just having trouble loving me right now."

Because children have no way of knowing that in other homes, or indeed in other cultures or eras, their behavior would not be judged wrong, they conclude that there is something wrong with them. This most basic error in thinking totally runs our lives from childhood to old age. It results in repressing our natural way of being and in our becoming approval seekers, trying to find the "right" way to be.

The truth is that parents get upset over the behavior of their children because it taps into some of the parents' fears, which come from their own beliefs. For example, when parents fear that children will grow up to be weak if they are held when they cry, parents will either ignore their crying or criticize them ("That's nothing to get upset about!") in an attempt to get their children to be strong. Children take this personally and feel wrong, since they can't know that they are okay and that any unloving behavior comes from their parents' difficulty in loving. In any case, the child winds up feeling unlovable. After years of the message that you're wrong when another person becomes upset with your behavior, is it any wonder why you have such a deep well of self-doubt? Everyone in the world suffers, to varying degrees, from this insecurity.

All your emotional fear stems from the belief that you're

inadequate or unlovable. Your defense system is built on this fear, and the defensiveness that follows it permeates everything in your life. You hold back, you become closed to learning, and your ability to love is severely crippled.

Although at one time you needed a strong defense system (a predominant ego), as an adult you no longer need this for survival. Unfortunately, by now it has become habitual and very powerful.

You've moved past your fears in some areas but have probably avoided the areas where your biggest fears lie. For example, a man with few fears of his athletic ability might develop strength and agility but avoid his intellectual development due to his belief that he is inadequate in that area. A woman, on the other hand, who has feelings of fear and inadequacy about taking care of herself financially might avoid development in that area.

The basic error in your thinking has led you to the belief that if you can get enough love, you will feel better about yourself. However, as we stated earlier, your feelings of self-worth cannot come from *getting* love but only from *giving* love. When you feel inadequate and unlovable, moving into being loving is a real challenge. The more secure you feel, the more loving you can be. The more you are in your ego, the more your self-esteem is eroded. It is important to note that your immediate reactions are almost always from your ego.

From your well of self-doubt spring your defensive protections. Taking things personally, you quickly lash back or withdraw, retreating behind your protections rather than opening to learning about both yourself and the other person. When criticized, made wrong, and so on, it's very difficult to remain open, curious, soft, and loving. Were you to know the truth—that in fact you are *not* bad or wrong—then you wouldn't get thrown off your center when another person gets upset with you.

Everyone's center is love. Covering that center are our protective behaviors, which come up whenever we get frightened. The more frightened the individual, the more protected he/she is. The Hitlers of the world are the most frightened of all. We need to protect ourselves from them without losing sight of the fact that even they are lovable at their cores. Admittedly that's a tall order, but it's something to shoot for. Meanwhile, you can start by loving those around you who are behaving in less hideous, but nonetheless unloving, ways. And, most important, you can learn to love yourself when you run into your own nonloving, judgmental ego.

How do you feel about your core? When do you judge yourself "wrong"? These are among the questions that will take you on a lifetime journey of learning by questioning the beliefs that limit your self-esteem, joy, and intimacy. Think about the things you were made wrong for. Were you wrong when you expressed sexual curiosity, a desire to play with dolls, or aggression, dreaminess, rebelliousness, or sensitivity? Were you made wrong because of how you looked, walked, spoke, or thought?

We all behave in unloving ways, at times—unloving to ourselves as well as to others. But your life can become so much better as you become less judgmental. What is the purpose of being judgmental? What is your fear of giving up being judgmental? It is the answer to this last question that will take you to the doorstep of some of your most basic self-limiting beliefs.

The ego contains hundreds of false, self-limiting beliefs. Some of the most prevalent, and the ones that lead to almost all of your unhappiness, are:

- You are bad, inadequate, unlovable, unworthy.

- Others are responsible for your feelings or actions. You are a victim, a helpless reactor, powerless over how you feel.

- You are responsible for others' feelings or actions.

- You will find happiness and/or inner peace outside of yourself from things such as money, sex, love, drugs or alcohol, approval, clothes, and power over others.

- Anger will get you what you want.

- Getting others to give you what you want will make you happy.

- You can't handle pain because you don't know how to find your way through the pain to joy.

When you believe you're wrong or inadequate, you have to protect yourself. To do this, you: (1) control others to keep their love; (2) give yourself up to keep their love; or (3) shut down to keep from having to deal with the fear of loss. The basic fear that runs our lives is the fear of loss—loss of another's love and/or loss of self (integrity, identity). Tied to this is the belief that we can't make ourselves happy and so we must depend on others for our happiness. The flip side of this coin is the equally false belief that we are responsible for others' feelings. As long as we operate from these beliefs, we are hopelessly entangled with and dependent on the people in our lives, stuck in a downward cycle, unable to move into our Higher Selves and to learn. We become like addicts, helplessly out of control in that area of our lives.

DEPENDENT RELATIONSHIPS IN AN ADDICTIVE SOCIETY

We have been well trained to become addicts. As children, very few of us were taught how to rely on ourselves for our happiness. Instead, we were raised to be dependent on things outside of ourselves for our good feelings. Everything from advertisements to love songs have taught us that someone or something will solve our problem for us— whether it's loneliness, alienation, unpopularity, or unhappiness. Or perhaps we discovered on our own that we could blot out our feelings by overeating, becoming mesmerized in front of the TV, having sex, popping a pill, or working excessively.

At the root of all dependency is our many self-limiting beliefs. The years of being told that what you want and feel are wrong has left you lost, seeking answers outside yourself, running from one pursuit to another in the search for happiness, satisfaction, peace, joy, intimacy, and love.

Co-dependent Relationships

Almost everybody believes that happiness comes from connecting to another person, and connection truly is a wonderful experience. However, when you need that person to make you feel whole, worthwhile, and happy, you are not being personally responsible and are not in your Higher Self. What happens with most people is that they don't know how to find themselves on the inside, so their unhappiness comes not from the lack of connection with another person but from the lack of connection with themselves.

Everything you've been taught says that love equals need, and the more you need, the greater your love. Every love song you've ever heard tells you things like: "Can't live, if living is without you. Can't give, can't give anymore"; "There's just no me without you." That's pretty drastic. The messages are: "My whole life is dependent on this relationship and without it, I'm nothing," or, "I was miserable until you came along and now I'm great," or, "I was happy until you left me and now I'm miserable and I'll stay that way the rest of my life."

The promise is that another person's giving you love will solve your problems, make you happy, give you the security you desire, make you feel good about yourself, and give you the vitality and clarity that you need to conquer the world. Love *does* have that power, but when you are dependent on another for happiness, you aren't being personally responsible, and that's not love. The problem is that you have been led to believe the fairy tale that when you find someone to love you, then and *only* then will you live happily ever after. A relationship based on this myth will disintegrate as both partners operate from the false belief that we don't have the right to make ourselves happy because we are flawed in some way, or that we don't have the power within us to take care of our own needs. When we don't know these beliefs are false, we need to have control over others. We become dependent on them for our good feelings (or to dull our pains—loneliness, boredom, unlovableness), and a co-dependent relationship is formed between takers and caretakers.

Takers

People whose primary fear is that they don't have the *power* to make themselves happy generally become takers. They believe that it's the other person's behavior that is making them unhappy, and that if only the other would change, things would be fine. Their manipulations are obvious as they attempt to control others by intimidating them with fear and guilt.

Caretakers

People whose primary fear is that they don't have the *right* to make themselves happy generally become caretakers. They are compliers, believing it's their responsibility to make others happy. When others are upset, they try to make things right by giving themselves up, hoping that by making others happy, they will be loved and therefore will be happy.

People become caretakers when they believe that others don't have the power to take care of themselves. They believe that others are fragile and see themselves as strong.

There are caretakers who don't know how to make themselves happy (these caretakers are often takers as well), and there are caretakers who do know how, but who must wait to make themselves happy until those around them are happy. (These are primarily martyrs.) Such caretakers' controlling is very subtle, but it is nevertheless manipulative and therefore unloving.

We all, at times, behave as caretakers and takers. However, many people become entrenched in one or the other of these roles, and unloving relationships are the result. Both categories of behavior are motivated by fear, and both roles are needy and focus on getting the other person's approval. Neither is loving.

To understand what love is and to become a truly loving person, you must be willing to deal with your dependence on other people. The beliefs that create the protections of being a taker or caretaker go very deep. Changing your role requires a major commitment to freeing yourself from your self-limiting beliefs and fears. Takers must learn how to make themselves happy; caretakers must be willing to risk losing another's love, either temporarily or permanently.

One of the most common fears in co-dependent relationships is being "wrong." To eliminate fear, you will have to take inventory of all your beliefs. (This is the focus of Section II.) You must take the time to discover what truly makes you happy and what you need to do to bring that about. You must develop faith, and that can occur only as you turn your life over more and more to the only thing greater than your ego mind—your Higher Self. The more you have faith in your Higher Self, the more personally powerful you become and the less you will need dependent connections. Then you will be free to connect with others in truly loving relationships.

Love is unconditional. Dependent, needy feelings always have strings attached. "I will love you if . . ." or, "If you really loved me, you would . . ." are the unspoken control mechanisms of conditional love. We give in order to get something: love, connection, approval, safety, sex, more communication, change, appreciation, and so on. The problem is not in our wanting such things—it's in our attempts to manipulate others to give us these things. All of our thinking is tied up in the unloving consciousness of the ego—to *get* love. Love is a rare commodity.

One of the greatest problems in our thinking about love is our belief that "love" means being a caretaker, being nice, giving when somebody doesn't want it, or giving when somebody is angry. But in truth, loving means loving *yourself*. What is loving to your Higher Self is automatically loving to others. This means taking responsibility for making yourself happy.

The way out of all this is to tune in to what really makes you feel good about yourself. It never increases your self-esteem to give in order to get. It doesn't work inside, because if the person doesn't react as you'd hoped, you're miserable. It does make you happy inside when you give because it feels good to do so.

People often say, "I've given and given and given and I have no more left to give." This usually indicates that they've given themselves up or they've given with strings attached, in order to get love, approval, connection, and so on. They continue to give because they feel empty and are trying to get others to fill them up. That is not loving. When you give without expectation of getting something in return, it always makes you feel wonderful. And that's love.

To be more loving, you must look at the barrier that keeps you from behaving that way. That barrier is *always* fear. As soon as you discover what the fear is and what false belief is causing it, you can find out where you got the belief, why you keep it, and, through the exercises in Section II, get rid of it.

Connecting with your Higher Self puts you on a spiritual path—the path to discover the truth. This path is the only way out of the problems created by your ego. Since joy, peace, love, and intimacy exist only when you are in your Higher Self, the more time you spend there, the better your life will be. Once you accept that there is a source of knowledge other than your ego, you can let go and let your Higher Self take over and guide you. You—and every other human being—have that inner knowing, that infallible guide that will tell you when you're off center, but it needs to be cultivated in order to emerge from the recesses into which it has been stuffed.

It's very frightening to open to a new way of thinking. We are very attached to our traditional ways. Retraining your inner voice from "How do I get love?" to "How do I give love?" will require an effort—and that is where your task lies. Many people will not entertain the notion of a Higher Self until their lives are in shambles. However, you don't have to reach a crisis to realize that you will never get what you want as long as your fears are in control. It's only through the love of our Higher Selves that we can bring about peace within ourselves, within our families, and on our planet.

We find such ideas as God is love . . . The kingdom of heaven lies within . . . Know thyself . . . To thine own self be true . . . *contain a universal truth: As we look inward and discover our natural selves, we become more loving human beings and therefore more one with God. Continuing explorations and deepening self-knowledge, then, give a special, compelling purpose to life — achieving harmony with our natural selves, with the God within us. The more we live with love, the more peaceful, flowing, and right we feel. When we drop our protections and connect with each other from our natural selves, we experience the spiritual dimension of Intimate Love.*

—Jordan and Margaret Paul,
from *Do I Have to Give Up Me to Be Loved by You?*

· 2 ·

OUR PERSONAL ODYSSEY—
UNTANGLING A
CO-DEPENDENT SYSTEM

Our spiritual pursuits and beliefs have become increasingly important to us. As with most people, it required a crisis for us to understand the importance of this aspect of our lives.

With all our knowledge and commitment, our marriage ran into its second critical period about four years ago. The first difficult period had occurred after eight years of marriage, and we documented it in *Free to Love*. We had learned a great deal from that period, and it had led to the creation of our Intention Training model. However, we hadn't recognized the underlying difficulties that continued to eat away at our intimacy. We had uncovered some of the aspects of our control-compliance system, but we hadn't gotten down to the more subtle issues that kept getting in the way of our experiencing joy and love. As we took a closer look at our system, we began to discover the very difficult patterns that had developed between us.

We had slipped into a co-dependent relationship, with Margie being responsible for the emotional health of the family. Thinking she was being loving, she had given up important parts of herself to make everyone else happy, and she felt increasingly hurt and angry when her efforts didn't produce appreciation and love. Jordan was raised to be taken care of, and he had made Margie responsible for his happiness and was always irritated and angry with her whenever he wasn't happy. He thought that when he wasn't happy it was because Margie wasn't sexual enough, funny enough, or *something* enough.

As Margie began to find her happiness outside of our relationship, she became less and less available, and all the kids— Sheryl, Josh, Eric, and Jordan—became very unhappy, blaming, and defensive.

When the self-righteous anger and blame subsided, we began to unravel the system of beliefs that was causing our unhappiness. Finally, each individual in the family looked at his/her part in creating the limiting system we were in. As a result, we all began discovering more and more about ourselves—the joyful parts that had become muted in our self-limiting roles. We are now beginning to feel better about ourselves and one another.

JORDAN

Margie's decision to pursue activities away from the family when she felt pulled at to make us happy, or when any of us was angry with her, was an act of love. She was giving us a gift of the truth—the truth that no one feels good about or wants to be around people who are unloving. If we don't let others know when we feel unloved, or if we simply leave unloving situations (emotionally or physically) without expressing our feelings, we perpetuate a system of lies. The truth is always a gift because it creates an opportunity to learn and to change. But people often don't appreciate the truth as a gift of love.

I reacted the way most people do when afraid of opening to the truth: I got angry and sought others' support as I complained about the unfairness of my situation. Have you ever heard yourself in the following dialogue:

"Can you believe what she's doing!"

"I don't blame you for being angry. I wouldn't stand for someone doing that to me."

"Yeah. Look at all I've done for her—and that's the thanks I get."

"I can't believe how selfish she's being."

"I don't know if I can take this. Maybe I should just find someone else who would appreciate me."

The kids and I self-righteously supported one another's complaints about Margie's withdrawal from us. Armed with such support, I stayed angry, waiting for her to "shape up." There was no intention to learn on anyone's part, so we were stuck in a deteriorating situation. The more I stayed angry, the more Margie stayed away; the more she was away, the more I was angry.

Finally, we realized that we were so deeply enmeshed in our system that we needed the help of objective friends and of therapists (some of whom we'd trained) to help us see the issues more clearly. As our system unraveled, we learned more about co-dependence and began to understand what we had created. What a rude awakening it was to realize that we were like addicts and that we needed to accept an ongoing process of recovery.

For me, the beginning was having to look at my sexual neediness and how obsessive my thinking had become. I now see that we all have grown up with many false beliefs about sex, which lead us to sexually related problems.

Most men have been conditioned to believe that their self-worth hinges on their being attractive to women. So, when a man is attracted to a woman and takes her out, getting her to have sex with him is usually his primary goal. He may take her to dinner, to a movie, talk with her about areas of interest—but if the evening doesn't wind up in bed, often he is frustrated and angry. He may feel bad about himself ("If I were more interesting, successful, better-looking, or funnier, she would have gone to bed with me"); he may feel used if she doesn't honor his unspoken contract ("I'll be nice to her and in return she'll give me sex"); he may even feel angry because she has denied him the opportunity to give her his wonderful gift, deluding himself into believing that his attempt to "give" to her is altruistic.

Earlier in my life, my major focus in relationships with women was to get sexual affirmation. When I wasn't happy and something was wrong, sex may not have been the cause, but I thought it would be the cure. That made Margie, as my wife and sexual partner, responsible for my happiness. I thought that if only she would initiate sex more often, be sexier, and want sex more often, then I'd be happy and we'd be happy.

Whenever I was unhappy, then, it was because she wasn't doing something right. I was often uptight with her and couldn't understand why she wasn't interested in me sexually. I wasn't ready to hear that her sexuality was directly connected with her feeling loved.

31

When Margie finally decided not to have sex with me unless she felt loved and loving, that was the last straw. I believed that if we waited for that to happen, we would never make love again. And how could I ever feel good about myself if my wife rejected me? Being trained to think in such ways, my mind raced ahead in self-righteous anger to the thought of finding someone else to make love with. After all, I deserved it, and Margie was wrong.

Night after night I'd toss and turn, alternately cursing her and thinking, "Here is this woman I have lusted over for twenty years. She is beautiful; she matches my most erotic fantasies. She's next to me in bed, naked—and I can't even touch her! *Why?* Why is this happening to me?" The answer to that question took me on a fascinating journey of confronting my beliefs about sex and learning the truth.

The Bible says that "the truth will set you free." Nowhere in my life has this been so dramatically demonstrated than in my discovering the truth about my sexuality. The false beliefs that imprisoned me and kept me unhappy were that I needed sex in order to feel good about myself, to sleep well at night, and to be loving with my wife and faithful to her. Another crippling false belief was that I had the right to get my needs met, and that a woman's right to say "no" was not as important. My momentary pleasure was worth any price, even if it meant Margie was temporarily unhappy. After all, I thought, more sex would cure the feeling of emptiness and distance between us.

As we went through months of very infrequent lovemaking, I had plenty of opportunity to discover these beliefs and test them out. One by one, they were brought into the light of truth.

When I look over these commonly held false beliefs and realize how much misery they caused us both, I feel very sad. Men have perpetuated many false beliefs about their own and women's sexuality—beliefs that have led to low self-esteem, marital problems, child abuse, and rape. Even in this enlightened age, false beliefs about sex are expressed all around us.

Knowing that I don't *need* sex has been very liberating. Yes, I still desire to connect sexually and love our sexual experiences. When they are an expression of our intimacy, they are beautiful and passionate. However, when we are not in an open and flowing place, my intention now is to resolve the problem that is causing our distance rather than to create a pseudo-closeness by having sex. When Margie is not feeling sexual, we can still be affectionate, and that's wonderful. Without my former urgency to complete the sexual act, many new options and freedoms open up to us.

While I was confronting my sexual neediness, it became apparent that I was excessively dependent on Margie in other ways, too. One evening before I was to leave on a trip, I said, "I'm going to miss you." Margie replied, "Why? I haven't been very nice to you lately and we haven't been getting along well."

I thought for a moment about the work I would be doing on my trip and the people I'd be working with. "You're right," I said. "I'm not going to miss you." Later that night, I thought about what I'd said and realized that in my belief system, if I really loved Margie I would have been miserable being away from her, since I needed her in order to be happy.

The next morning I talked with Margie about my realization of how love was all tied up with need. I blurted, "But if I didn't need you, why would I be with you?" "Because we like being together and we offer each other some wonderful things," she answered.

I quickly realized that it is impossible to love someone or something you need for your happiness or well-being. Neediness feels weak and eventually turns into resentment toward the person or thing you need. The alcoholic doesn't love alcohol any more than the compulsive eater loves food. The desperate energy of need is the antithesis of love. Yet, our culture teaches us the "romantic love" of neediness.

I further realized why I got angry every time we reunited after having been separated. While I spoke of missing Margie and not being very happy during our time apart, and she would speak enthusiastically about the wonderful time she had had, I was sure that this meant that I loved her more than she loved me, and I would get sullen and withdrawn.

That morning I discussed this, too, with Margie. She became

very excited as we talked and said, "Maybe this time we can each have a wonderful time while we're apart, and when we get back together we can share our excitement." What a novel thought! We kissed good-bye.

I came back happy, she shared with me the good time she'd had, I felt happy for her, and our shared joyous intimacy created one of the best evenings of our lives.

That was the beginning of my confronting one of my deepest beliefs—that I couldn't make myself happy. I had depended on Margie, just as a child depends on a parent, to take care of me emotionally. To the outside world I'm sure I didn't look needy. I was successful and self-assured in both my professional and social activities. But at home I was a needy child depending on "mommy" to make me happy. Of course, I could entertain myself with reading, television, or work, but I was always secretly waiting for the time Margie and I would spend together.

What did it mean to be able to be happy on my own, to find joy in anything I was doing? I had never considered that before. It would mean that I'd be happy both when I was with Margie and when I was not.

There were not many things I did without her in which I found joy, and I knew I had to find more of them. But the deeper issue was how to find joy in *whatever* I was doing. I was familiar with that concept from some of my readings in Zen philosophy.

At this point I began to confront the meaning of God and my Higher Self. One day during this period I went out to our backyard to read, and I found myself experiencing reading not just to fill time, but actually experiencing joy in reading. As the sun warmed me and the slight breeze caressed the hair on my body, I felt my whole being become filled with the beauty of the environment we had created, and I was overwhelmed with the beauty that God had created without any help from me. It was a spectacular experience . . . and Margie wasn't even there! But could I do that in every moment of my life? It would be a major challenge, but I could at least start by making it happen more often. It was then that I realized that the things around me didn't change; it was my beliefs that changed.

The changes were not easily accomplished. I had to test out my fear of not needing her. If we were that free, would we still have a marriage? That freedom is one of the most frightening things for couples to confront.

I came to understand how I had become dependent on Margie taking care of me emotionally. Like most men, I had been taken care of by my mother, who I believed was responsible for my happiness and unhappiness. And then I grew up and got married to . . . guess who?

Because of our early dependence on our mothers, most men have deep, basic fears of women. That issue rarely gets resolved in childhood and so must be dealt with in our adult relationships with women. The fear began when we needed both our mothers' love and our own identities at the same time. Since needing Mother was terrifying, we developed a love-hate relationship with her. As I reflect on my work with men, it seems to me that this ambivalence men grow up with toward women leads to six distinct behaviors: (1) being attracted to women we can control; (2) staying away from relationships altogether; (3) being drawn to relationships with men (these are men who seem to become homosexual out of fear rather than actual preference or predisposition); (4) giving up and allowing women to be dominant; (5) keeping a number of women available to us—not putting all our eggs in one basket; and (6) being attracted to powerful women and then getting into power struggles with them out of our fear of being controlled by them.

The last item is the pattern I had always created. I am very attracted to powerful women, but being in a relationship with one taps into my deepest fears, and then up come my defenses. I used to daydream about how nice it would be to be married to Suzie Homemaker, but I have never been attracted to that kind of woman. My best alternative? Keep Margie and resolve my fears of being powerful enough to have an equal relationship in which I don't have to be in control to prevent being controlled. (The need to be in control always comes from the fear of being controlled. It can be hard to see, but people who seem to be controlling and powerful are actually afraid and weak.)

As I began my spiritual studies, I became fascinated with those people who were truly powerful, who didn't have to be controlling because they came from a place of sureness inside themselves. The power that comes with that sureness is awesome. That's how I wanted to be. I didn't want to have to control either subtly or overtly. I wanted to be able to stay centered in any situation, no matter how my wife or my children or anyone else behaved.

I began to study Jesus. Not the Jesus who has been distorted to meet the ego needs of men, but the Jesus who was the model of love, who reacted to all situations with love. Although not a member of any particular church or movement, I am continuing to search for the inner knowledge that will help me to be the best person I can.

What gets in the way of that are my false, self-limiting beliefs. The most pervasive result of those beliefs is feeling wrong. The fear of being wrong destroys every opportunity I have to learn and change. The fear of being wrong is what keeps us all from being open to learning. In any situation, I completely lose the desire to learn when I fear that in the learning I'll find out that I'm inadequate— *wrong*. Only when I take full responsibility for my life can I open to learning. When I don't take full responsibility because I fear being wrong, I get stuck focusing on Margie's part in the difficulty rather than staying focused on myself. When responsibility means blame, I'm stuck. This area of my work has created the most profound, transforming changes. These changes come not from a decision to change but from the changes in beliefs that move me from my ego to my Higher Self.

I feel best about myself when I react with openness, caring, and love. I feel alive, powerful, in control. When I am protected— defensive, pulled in, tight, attempting to control—I feel dead, weak, and scared. It's hardest to maintain my center when I'm with Margie. It's always in our primary relationships that our biggest challenge lies. But nothing is more important in my life than learning to be loving, to move into the consciousness that touches in a positive way everyone I meet.

MARGIE

I've always believed that it takes two people to create problems in a relationship, but tuning in to my end of the responsibilities has been difficult. I'd always seen myself as the giving one in the relationship, so how could my actions be causing the problems?

One of the clues I had was that I was not happy. I knew intellectually that if I were being truly loving and giving from my heart, I would feel happy and joyful—but it wasn't working out that way. The giving, which often came from fear of Jordan's withdrawal or guilt over feeling responsible for his happiness and unhappiness—was very draining to me. I was generally tired and often sick. And no matter how much I gave, Jordan never seemed to get enough. He wasn't happy, either.

Jordan and I had established our patterns even before we got married. I had always experienced myself as competent—able to fix things, get things done, and get what I wanted. Jordan, on the other hand, saw himself as a "spectacular failure" at everything he had tried. Yet, I saw him as a man with "great potential" for caring and sensitivity. He seemed, at the beginning, available for the kind of intimate marriage and family I wanted. I wanted children very much, I had been dating many different men for a long time, and I wanted to settle down.

We had known each other only a few weeks when he withdrew the first time. I was dismayed, but I jumped into the caretaker role I had always known and created the safe space for him to open. This was the beginning of a pattern that continued until recently. The more I jumped in to caretake, the more he withdrew, and the more he withdrew, the more I became a caretaker. I did the same thing with his anger: I would rush in to find out what he was angry at and what I could do to fix it.

It took me a long time to recognize my responsibility for the problems in our family. After all, I had prided myself on being the giver; I went along with what people wanted and always tried to fix their problems. On the surface that looks loving, but when I saw how often my behavior was motivated by fear and guilt, and how it was neither giving others personal responsibility for their lives nor taking responsibility for myself, I was shocked.

My identity and self-worth were tied up in being a caretaker. I put my needs last, believing that what I wanted wasn't important and that I did not have the right to make myself happy. Being a caretaker was how I had learned to get approval in childhood. I had been a "good" little girl by either repressing who I was or expressing it without letting my parents know. I believed I was responsible for their happiness or unhappiness and was forever adjusting my behavior either to make them happy or keep them from becoming unhappy. I was, in short, addicted to approval.

When I began to confront the price I paid for my compliance, I realized how burdened I felt with the responsibilities I had taken on. And no matter how much I did for others, they never seemed to get enough. I felt depleted and unhappy most of the time, and I didn't like myself, but I was terrified to confront the problems. I thought that if I was honest about how unhappy I was, Jordan and our family might fall apart. I believed I was the glue, and my terror was in testing that out.

One of the deepest fears I have had to confront was that if I behaved as who I really am, from my Higher Self, others would be upset with me and withdraw their love. I had lived with that false, painful belief my whole life.

In the beginning of our relationship, as I proceeded to "fix" Jordan, he seemed to blossom. He became successful, more self-assured, even more sensitive. Most people loved him, but with me he was often shut down and seemed angry. Naturally, I believed that if I could fix the things in me that "made him" unhappy, our relationship would get better. What I failed to see at that time was that Jordan and I were colluding to make me responsible for his happiness.

The more I gave up myself, the more unhappy I became—and the more Jordan felt angry with me. By having him be dependent on me, I was partially responsible for keeping him an emotional cripple and that was *not* loving. I still feel pain when I look back at that behavior.

I have always received a lot of criticism for the way I think and act. Twenty-five years ago, my ideas about nutrition—I ate natural, chemical-free foods—were criticized as kooky. As an artist, my most creative time was at night, so I often painted till dawn and slept until noon. In graduate school, both my subjects and my colors were criticized by my instructors. Like the "good girl" I'd learned to be, I covered up who I really was and how I really felt.

I always felt a tremendous inner conflict between who I really was and what others expected of me. In my marriage, whenever the "unusual" part of me would surface, Jordan would get upset, we would argue, and then usually I would give up wanting what I wanted or doing what I wanted—but it never changed my desires.

Even though I gave in a lot, I also continually brought up the subjects on which we were at odds—issues of nutrition, sexuality, emotions, metaphysics, spirituality, and so on. My intention was to get Jordan to open and to change—"for his own good," of course. Most discussions wound up in power struggles. I never understood why he got so defensive whenever I wanted to talk, until I recognized that my intention was to get him to change and he was resisting being controlled by me. It was quite shocking to me to see how controlling I was.

I realized that I needed to think differently. But this didn't come easily. Since my feelings and behavior were never motivated by the intention to hurt another, why were my feelings or behavior wrong? What *really* caused others to feel hurt? When I finally took a deep look, I realized that feelings come from beliefs. Therefore, I could never *cause* other people to feel a certain way; rather, *their* beliefs were causing their feelings. If a person believed something was wrong, he or she would get upset. If I didn't want to make love with Jordan and he got hurt, then his hurt was coming from *his* fears and beliefs. If I jumped up and down when I was excited and this embarrassed him, his upset came from his beliefs about "appropriate" behavior and his fears of others' judging him by my behavior. It was liberating to realize that this applied to everything that we have come to believe is the "right way" to be. As long as my intention is not to harm another person, is there any behavior that is wrong?

At first I took my newfound freedom with some hard self-righteousness. But now I know that whenever I get hard and irritated, it's because I'm afraid that someone—especially Jordan—can make me feel guilty and talk me out of my feelings. Confronting my irritation has been extremely important for my growth. Obviously, the more secure I feel, the softer I can remain. Real strength comes from knowing that it's okay to feel what I feel and want what I want.

I tested out my freedom in many areas and learned a lot from each. One of the most profound learnings has occurred in the area of sexuality. Both Jordan and I have been astounded about how many erroneous beliefs we grew up with about sex. I never knew that I had the right not to be touched or made love to if I didn't want to. I was afraid that any man with whom I was involved would be upset with me if I didn't allow him to use my body—or that if he was upset with me, he might feel inadequate, and I would be responsible for that.

I felt there was something wrong with me if I didn't feel aroused as often as Jordan. I felt there was something wrong with me for sometimes not wanting Jordan to touch me, and in not appreciating how much he enjoyed looking at and making love to my body.

It has taken me a long time to appreciate and validate my sexuality, which is very different from Jordan's. Neither one is wrong, we're just different. He has had a greater physical need for sex than I do. In addition, my sexuality is much more connected to my emotions than his, although recently that has changed a great deal for him. For me, sex is the outgrowth of feeling emotionally connected and loving. I need to be connected emotionally *before* I feel sexual. Jordan, on the other hand, opens emotionally much more easily *after* we make love.

It's been difficult for me not to feel guilty and wrong for not wanting sex much as men have wanted me to. In the past, I often gave in and had sex when I wasn't turned on in order to avoid a man's anger, or to please him, or to protect him from feeling bad. Sex was totally tied up with guilt and fear. As I realized this, I began to wonder what it would be like if sex happened as a result of love and mutual desire rather than neediness.

As I've become more aware of the good reasons I have for

feeling as I do, I've realized that there are two different kinds of touch—either a giving or a taking. Sometimes I feel Jordan's touch as caring and nurturing, and it feels wonderful. But at other times his touch is trying to *get* something from me—to get me aroused, to appreciate him, to take comfort for himself. When this happens I feel invaded and used, because he's caring only about himself.

Sex, too, is either nurturing or taking. Unfortunately, sex is usually either taking (using) or giving in (being used). We've been trained since childhood to use these two ways of expressing ourselves sexually. Sex as a giving, loving experience is, sadly, quite rare.

Jordan has come to realize that a great deal of his sex drive was out of neediness rather than love. When he finally acknowledged this and opened to learning about it, we experienced an important turning point in our relationship.

He recently tuned in to the fact that he has been using me as a conduit to connect to himself. He seems to get to his softness, openness, lovingness, and pain *through* me—through my touch or softness. Since this still feels as if he's making me responsible for his openness to learning, I usually choose not to be with him unless he is already willing to be open.

I am very attuned to people's energy. When Jordan is shut down and silently angry, I can feel that coldness in another part of the house. In the past, when I'd offer him my perceptions, he'd tell me that he wasn't shut down—he would say essentially that I was crazy. I didn't have enough confidence in myself to know that I was right. Now I know that when I'm sensing something, I may not always label it correctly, but something's going on. For example, when I feel Jordan's uptight energy I may say, "You seem angry." If he says, "I'm not angry," then we're stuck—he's not open to learning and there's no place to go. If he says, "I'm not aware of feeling angry but let's take a look at what you're sensing and what I'm feeling," then we can learn, and my perception that something's going on is validated.

I feel the difference between Jordan's sexual energy when he's needy and when he's caring. I feel the difference between the energy of his openness and his closedness. When people pull at me for approval, the energy I feel is completely different from that of people who possess real inner strength. I also feel the distinctly different energies between victims and those who take personal responsibility for themselves. As I learn to trust my perceptions more, some people get very uncomfortable—in particular, those who are not open to learning. I truly love to learn. I am excited by the challenges in learning. I experience crisis as an opportunity to learn and I seek new challenges to increase my learning. To me, the most important purpose in life is to be loving and to learn about the blocks to loving.

I would rather learn than teach. Jordan loves to teach, but learning has been difficult for him, because of his fears of being wrong. So, our learning has not always been fun, nor has it been the wonderfully joyful process that it can be. But we *have* learned a lot together.

When we are both open to learning, the intimacy and growth that become possible are incredible. Any situation can create intimacy or distance, depending upon whether we approach it with the intent to learn or the intent to protect.

Many interesting and challenging things have resulted in our lives as a result of my respecting my right to follow my own path. Jordan and I have begun to do many more things separately. He does most of the professional teaching and writing. I do more therapy and spend a great deal more time pursuing my art, as well as writing separately from him. Art has become an important vehicle for me to delve more deeply into my femininity. Being alone is much more important to me than it is to Jordan, and I've recently come to respect my need to be alone.

My decision to respect my need to be alone and to pursue these separate activities has presented our latest, and perhaps most difficult conflict in our relationship yet. We are now challenged to apply the process of learning and loving behavior as we explore new and sometimes painful questions, such as, what if one partner has a change in personal or professional direction? Or what if one partner wants to change the structure or form of the relationship, given new learnings, while the other was fulfilled and satisfied with the status quo?

Jordan and I continue to struggle with these very fundamental relationship questions, and while the risks are real and the future not always clear, still the principles of loving behavior continue to be validated as we work through these latest problems together in search of answers for both of us.

We are certainly not out of the woods. The road has been very rocky but we're each much happier within ourselves, feeling stronger, more alive, more in harmony and integrity with who we really are. The struggle to change a deeply ingrained system could not have been accomplished without a great deal of help. Our friends, the therapists and writers who have helped us through their own willingness to struggle, and our spiritual teachers have been invaluable.

We must not forget one other important source of our growth—God. We were very nonreligious people for most of our lives, so perhaps our God is different from yours. It doesn't matter, really, what method you use to tap into the universal truth, as long as you understand that it is necessary to do so if we are to transcend the pitfalls created by human beings. To understand what it means to turn our lives over to our Higher Selves has been essential for us.

BOTH OF US

JORDAN: In the process of learning about our fears and beliefs, we are changed. As we change, whatever problem we were having will be changed and we will reach a mutually satisfying resolution. The concept of being in a process is very foreign to Westerners because we are very solution oriented. We don't have faith that if we just open to learning, we'll find resolution. Instead, we try to find solutions, or we go to other people who tell us what to do, calling them on the radio to be told in six minutes how to solve our problems. That's going right to solution rather than being in a process of growth and learning.

MARGIE: What keeps people from finding their resolutions

43

quickly is the power struggle—trying to be right. Nor can you reach resolution without genuinely caring about what the other person wants.

JORDAN: Some people really love the process of learning and it becomes a major part of their lives. Margie is that kind of person. I, on the other hand, am the kind of person who opens to learning only when I'm hit over the head and am forced to do it. However, once I've opened, I can experience the excitement of learning in any situation around me.

MARGIE: What I want in my life is to be with people who really want to learn. To many women, learning is the most important thing. But most men are afraid to be in that process.

JORDAN: That's true—men have been brought up to see *doing* as important, while women are much more able to just *be*. I don't know that I will ever get to the point where the process of being open to learning is as exciting to me as it is to Margie. So it may never be equal. But we can, and often do, find a balance, and that allows ever greater learning and deeper intimacy. And when Margie needs more learning and openness than I can share with her, she can get those needs met with other people.

MARGIE: But I don't need to be in the process of learning all the time. What I need is the *energy* of the openness. Just the *willingness* to be there when it's appropriate, and not run up against the wall. When the wall is there, there is no intimacy. I don't like to sit and process and learn all the time. I like to have fun and play. But that can't happen if there is a wall. It only happens when that energy of openness is there.

When two people are open, they don't have to

process very much at all. They need to process only when they are closed and protected and they need to find out why.

JORDAN: So our task is admittedly a very challenging one. Some of you may be thinking, "They're saying that if we do this, something wonderful is going to happen, but I've never had it so I don't even know what that feels like." But we know that it *does* happen. We've had enough experience to know that when that openness is there between us, the energy there is something really special. What follows—the joy and sexuality—is even more special. We define it as a spiritual connection. This process continues to teach us what it means to be truly loving to ourselves and to others. It has deepened our commitment to discovering what it will take to bring about peace within ourselves and our families, and finally, peace on our planet. We hope you are moved to join us.

COMES THE DAWN

After a while you learn the subtle difference
between holding a hand and chaining a soul,

And you learn that love doesn't mean leaning
and company doesn't mean security,

And you begin to learn that kisses aren't contracts
and presents aren't promises,

And you begin to accept your defeats with your head up
and your eyes open with the grace of a woman,
not the grief of a child,

And you learn to build all your roads on today
because tomorrow's ground is too uncertain for plans
and the future has a way of falling down in mid-flight.

After a while you learn that even sunshine
burns if you get too much,

So you plant your own garden and decorate your own soul
instead of waiting for someone to bring you flowers,

And you learn that you really can endure,

That you really have worth,

And you learn and you learn . . .

   With every goodbye

   With every sunset

   Comes the dawn.

—Jo Anne Kurman

47

INTRODUCTION TO SECTION II

The remainder of this workbook is designed to help you learn how to learn from conflicts. Since conflict occurs in all relationships, relationships are obviously a most important vehicle in your personal growth. The exercises are designed to be used for conflicts with anyone who is presently in your life or has been in your life, living or dead. You can learn from conflicts in adult love relationships (heterosexual or homosexual), relationships with your parents, children, employers, employees, business partners and clients, friends, relatives and even with yourself.

The exercises will give you the opportunity to learn about yourself on a very deep level and can be used over and over again to continually deepen your learning. This workbook is probably different from any other workbook you may have used because each exercise is related to a concept about learning.

Chapter 3, "Loving Behavior," contains exercises for beginning to think about and look for loving behavior. This thinking is the unusual and crucial shift in consciousness that will transform your life.

Chapter 4, "Basic Learning Skills," contains formats for exploration to help you remove the blocks to being a more loving person. You can use these formats anytime you're open to learning from your conflicts. The formats will help you focus on the questions you can ask yourself over and over again to find the answers to what's causing your unhappiness and to find the way out of that unhappiness. All of the exercises in this book are designed to help you use these formats.

When you are stuck in your protections, the exercises in Chapter 5, "Moving Out of Protection," will help you become open to learning.

Being aware of what you do in a conflict and the consequences that follow from your behavior is an important part of your motivation to change. Chapter 6, "Protections and Consequences," contains many exercises to deepen your learning about your protections and their consequences.

Being open to learning means being open to learning about the fears that are in the way of your being a loving person. Chapter 7, "Acknowledging and Respecting Fear," contains exercises that are designed to help you understand your fears, the first step in moving through them.

There are three healing exercises in Chapter 8, "Healing." These exercises are well worth your time and effort. Healing the wounds from your past is invaluable in unwrapping protective coverings.

Chapter 9, "Continuing the Process," contains ideas for learning with other people, by both helping others and receiving help from others. Other resources are also included for your continued learning.

USING THE SELF-LIMITING BELIEFS CHECKLISTS

We have included many checklists for discovering the beliefs that limit the expression and development of your potential. We are forever grateful to Wayne Dyer for popularizing this idea in *Your Erroneous Zones*. We use "erroneous," "false" and "self-limiting" interchangeably.

A belief is self-limiting and erroneous if it:

- keeps you from feeling good about yourself, happy, satisfied, successful;
- creates any negative feelings—fear, doubt, pain, depression, unhappiness, anxiety or guilt;
- diminishes self-esteem, self-worth, aliveness;
- makes you feel wrong, bad, inadequate.

Nonlimiting beliefs are those which:

- increase the quality of your life;
- increase your joy, happiness, self-esteem, dignity, lovability, health, feelings of fullness and aliveness;
- help you meet life with positive appreciation.

Anytime you are in pain of any sort, including anxiety and tension, you are operating from an erroneous belief. If you were not operating from that belief, you would not be in pain. And so, anytime you are in pain, it is possible to use that pain as an opportunity to learn. You can say, "What is the belief that I'm operating from that is bringing about this pain?" Obviously, if you are unwilling to feel your pain, if you are protected, you can't utilize your pain to learn, and you will just keep doing the very things that bring about the pain. Anytime you're upset, anytime you're not feeling joyful, know that there is self-limiting belief causing it.

On each list, check off the ones that you believe even a little bit. For example, your intellect may tell you that the belief "Women are not as intelligent as men" is not true, but if any part of you believes that, then check it. You can use these checklists to better understand your behavior and feelings. Work these lists from the child within you, rather than from your rational adult. Each checklist contains only a portion of the self-limiting beliefs in any area. If you become aware of beliefs that are not on the list, be sure to add them and we'd appreciate your sharing them with us. Each belief can be the subject of an exploration.

SHARING

At various places in the workbook, we have included conversations. This "sharing" dialogue is from Intention Training workshop participants during the workshop, along with our responses. We have included them where we thought it might help you become more aware of your thoughts and feelings.

TOGETHER OR ALONE

Most of the exercises in this workbook are designed to be done alone. Although almost every relationship problem is a result of a system created by two or more people, it only takes one person to break the system. You don't need others to learn about yourself.

Some of the exercises can be done either alone or with another person and there are two sets of instructions for those. There are a few exercises that can only be done with another person, but don't let that concern you. You can save them until you develop a friendship that feels safe enough to work together.

When we refer to your "partner," that's your partner for the exercise. This could be anyone with whom you feel comfortable.

In doing exercises with another person, it's important that you monitor your intention. It's very easy when working with a "significant other" to slip into being focused on getting that person to see things *you* think are important.

It's also important to follow the instructions for each exercise. We suggest you do an exercise for ten minutes. People often run out of things to say after about three or four minutes, and the fear that they won't be able to come up with anything more to say can raise a barrier to learning. If you start discussing the exercise or analyzing it or each other, you will miss the opportunity to go deeper into the exercise and the learning. The ego is very adept at enticing you into intellectual discussions which take you away from the deep learning that can occur on an emotional level. Of course, you will also find that you can enhance your learning by tailoring some exercises to your own particular needs. There is no single "right" way. Find the way that maximizes your learning.

CREATING THE OPTIMAL ENVIRONMENT

Before doing any exercises, check to see if it is the right time and place for you to do it. Create a space where you will be free of any intrusions from people, noises or other demands from the outside world. The desire to look into yourself and your past experience with a gentle and caring intention is a good beginning, but you also need to have the freedom to do your exploration without being interrupted. Also make sure you really want to learn. There is a right time and place for you. Is this it? If so, let's go forward.

FAITH

When you have come to the edge
of all the light you know,

And are about to step off
into the darkness of the unknown,

Faith is knowing
one of two things will happen:

There will be something solid to stand on,
or you will be taught how to fly.

—Anonymous

·3·

LOVING BEHAVIOR

Finding the loving behavior in a conflict isn't easy, since you haven't been taught to think in those terms. The odds are that most of your reactions in conflicts have been unloving. If the beliefs and fears of your ego were not in the way, loving behavior would flow naturally from your Higher Self. But that is not how we've been raised.

Behavior motivated by love is the exact opposite of the behavior modeled by the "heroes" of our society—business executives, athletes, movie "tough guys," the people who will do anything to "win." Loving behavior is the exact opposite of what we've seen in the world. It is people reacting openly rather than protectively and defensively. That is real power.

The following pages contain a "Definition of Loving Behavior," which will help you determine if your behavior is loving. We suggest that you photocopy it and keep it nearby so that you can refer to it frequently.

1. A DEFINITION OF LOVING BEHAVIOR

Loving behavior nurtures your own and others' emotional and spiritual growth, promotes personal responsibility, and increases your self-esteem.

It is behavior that is:

> Honest to yourself about yourself.
> Nonjudgmental of yourself and others.
> Harmonious with your Higher Self (rather than with your ego).
> Integrious (our own word, which means "behaving with integrity").
> Never invested in the outcome of an action.

It is the behavior that leaves you feeling:

Inner peace	Joyful	God-like
Unique, special	Lovable	Soft and strong
In control of yourself		

It is not the behavior that leaves you feeling:

Tense, anxious	Angry	Weak
Scared, unsure	Rigid	Blaming
Righteous, justified	Victimized	Stagnant

Unloving behavior is any attempt to:

Avoid taking personal responsibility by giving in
   or shutting down.
Take responsibility for others.
Get others to change.
Make others wrong.
Get others to give themselves up or doubt themselves.
Establish power over others.

Loving behavior:

Makes you feel the best about you—that you're adequate and
   worthwhile.
Is not motivated by fear or guilt.
Is not the safe, habitual path of least resistance, the rut you've
   fallen into—rescuer/rescued; taking care of/being taken care of.
Will often feel like the most difficult choice.
Will often challenge deeply held beliefs and fears.
Involves the risk that those who want you to take responsibility
   for their behavior, or want to control you, will not
   appreciate your efforts.
May be exactly opposite what you've been doing to gain
   approval or avoid disapproval (your own or others').

Behavior that nurtures your emotional and spiritual growth always nurtures the emotional and spiritual growth of others. It means caring and understanding without giving yourself up. It gives others the true gift of love—the opportunity to look honestly at themselves and to take personal responsibility.

The intent of unloving behavior is to get something: approval, love, affirmation, connection, safety, attention, a response, a change and so on.

The intent of loving behavior is to give. There are no strings, conditions or expectations attached.

The key to knowing whether your behavior is loving is how you wind up feeling about yourself and the consequences of your behavior. Loving behavior is the best that is within you.

When you are being loving and another person responds to you with love, intimacy will occur. Since you can't control how another chooses to react, there's never any guarantee. But there *is* a guarantee when you respond protectively: there will be no intimacy.

Your focus can always be inward, taking responsibility for your own growth and joy. Loving behavior is Selfish rather than selfish. Behavior that comes from the ego is selfish; it is concerned only with getting others to give to you and to love you, rather than giving to yourself and others. When behavior comes from the Higher Self, it is Selfish.

This new definition of loving behavior may have triggered many, many self-limiting beliefs.

THE INTENT TO LEARN IS ALWAYS LOVING.

Exercise 1A   Checklist—Self-limiting Beliefs That Get in the Way of Loving Behavior

In this and the following exercises, we have listed some of the most basic and important self-limiting fears and beliefs. They are obstacles to your behaving in a loving manner. Check off the ones that apply to you. We suggest that you review these beliefs often, using your responses to touch off your deepest philosophical and spiritual learning. A format for challenging your beliefs can be found in exercise 7, page 89.

___ 1. If I'm open to listening and learning, I will get talked out of my own views and feelings.

___ 2. If I'm open to learning, I will find out that I'm unlovable/inadequate.

___ 3. If I'm open to learning, I will get blamed for someone else's unhappiness and then I will have to change to make him/her happy.

___ 4. I can't make myself happy if someone around me is protecting him/herself.

___ 5. If I forgive the people who hurt me, they will just keep hurting me.

___ 6. If I forgive myself, then I will continue to do the things that hurt myself and others.

___ 7. If I'm soft and open, people will see me as weak and will lose respect for me.

___ 8. If I'm open and trusting, I'll get sucked in and duped. Then people will think I'm stupid and reject me.

___ 9. I can't handle rejection. I can't handle the pain.

___ 10. If I open to learning I will find out that everything is my fault, that I am the wrong one.

___ 11. If I open to learning then I will find out that what I'm doing isn't working and I will have to change.

___ 12. If I open to learning then I will have to face the fact that I am responsible for my unhappiness.

___ 13. Even if I open to my pain, nothing will change, so why bother?

Exercise 1B   Checklist—Self-limiting Beliefs about Loving Behavior

Loving means:

___ 1. Giving yourself up.

___ 2. Sacrificing your freedom, being a martyr.

___ 3. Taking responsibility for other's feelings.

___ 4. Not doing anything that another reacts to with pain.

___ 5. Being dependent, being needy.

___ 6. Needing each other for self-esteem.

___ 7. Withholding your truth if it hurts another.

___ 8. Coddling the other's ego.

___ 9. Giving sympathy when the other is a complaining victim.

___ 10. Protecting the other from ever feeling hurt or scared.

___ 11. Never walking away from another, even if he/she is abusive.

___ 12. Trying to get another to see the light.

___ 13. Rescuing, fixing another.

___ 14. Being miserable when you're not together.

___ 15. Being miserable when the other is miserable.

___ 16. Having sex.

___ 17. When other person makes him/herself happy when you're apart, he/she doesn't love you.

___ 18. If someone is not as miserable as you when you're apart, he/she doesn't love you.

___ 19. If your partner wants to be with another person rather than with you, he/she doesn't love you.

Exercise 1C Checklist—Self-limiting Beliefs about Love Relationships

___ 1. If I do what I need to do for myself to make myself happy, the other person will leave me.

___ 2. If I help another person feel good he or she will leave me.

___ 3. I have to give myself up to make the other person happy or the other person won't love me.

___ 4. Love is transitory, it can't last.

___ 5. No matter what I do, I'll always get hurt in the end.

___ 6. If I am myself, he/she won't accept me, will reject me.

___ 7. It's not possible to maintain both love and personal freedom.

___ 8. I'll always end up giving more than I get.

___ 9. When I love someone I'm responsible for their happiness.

___ 10. If someone really loves me, he/she would never do things that upset me.

___ 11. Love is imprisoning.

___ 12. You're one up or one down—either in control or being dominated.

___ 13. Close relationships lead to pain and rejection.

___ 14. You can't let another person be too important to you or you'll give yourself up or be rejected.

___ 15. I'll always be abandoned in the end.

___ 16. Getting rejected is the worse thing that can happen to me.

___ 17. (For women) If I am a successful and powerful woman, I won't be loved and I will end up alone.

___ 18. If I'm soft and gentle, people will see me as weak and I won't be loved.

___ 19. If only I have one person who is everything to me and to whom I am everything, then I will be happy.

___ 20. If I take care of myself, I cannot take care of another and vice versa—only one person gets taken care of.

___ 21. Aging will cause me to be abandoned and alone.

___ 22. If someone loves me, I ought to love him/her or I'm a bad person.

___ 23. I should let the other person set the pace of intimacy.

2. YOUR HIGHER SELF

Loving behavior is always loving to yourself. But unless you understand the difference between the ego and the Higher Self, it's possible to use that statement to support your ego-centered behavior. Many people have done this with disastrous results. Taking care of your ego self will never make you happy, for that behavior is selfish, self-centered, protected—the opposite of loving. Taking care of your Higher Self is Selfish. It leaves you feeling at peace and at one with yourself. It is real inner strength. It is the behavior that, in the face of a conflict, makes you feel secure enough to open. It is the behavior that increases your self-esteem and makes you feel stronger rather than weaker. It is not the false strength that comes when people "win"; beating others emotionally or physically just makes their egos stronger. So in order to understand what it means to "take care of yourself," it is essential that you understand which self you are taking care of.*

It is important to recognize times when you've been in harmony with your Higher Self and remember how you felt. All of us have, at times, been in harmony with our Higher Selves. The problem is that those times are so infrequent (relative to our ordinary experience) that many of us don't readily remember them. We also tend to dismiss those experiences as accidental or as unavailable to us on a regular and easily accessible basis. But this quality of being is available to you on a much greater scale and with far greater ease than you would believe. Further, we have found that to the degree you recover your memory of those times when you were operating from your Higher Self, you strengthen to the same degree your ability to re-create that quality of experience in the present or whenever you choose.

In *How Can I Help*? Ram Dass and Paul Gorman describe experiences of being in the Higher Self:

> So we look for and cherish those experiences in which we feel ourselves connected to all things in the universe.
>
> Out under the stars, stretching to encompass notions of distance and galaxies, "light years," until the mind just boggles and goes "tilt"—and suddenly your sense of specialness or separateness is replaced by a feeling of identity with the all inclusive immensity of the universe.
>
> Listening to a Bach chorale and feeling transported into a sense of order and harmony far beyond the music itself.
>
> Harvesting the garden, smiling as you remember the spring planting, and appreciating the lawfulness of fruition in nature, the same life energy in you.
>
> Making love, when you suddenly merge with someone very dear; two become one and you somehow feel more truly yourself than you ever had before.
>
> Or in service itself—comforting a crying child, reassuring a frightened patient, bringing a glass of water to a bedridden elder—when you feel yourself to be a vehicle of kindness, an instrument of love. There's more to the deed than the doer and what's been done. You yourself feel transformed and connected to a deeper sense of identity.

The following poem, written by Jordan, was an important step in his understanding of his Higher Self and illustrates the experience we're describing.

WHERE IS GOD?

I have always looked for a sign of the presence of God.
Was God here today?

Before the sun broke, I did
Into gales of laughter.
Bodies entwined, we giggled over my funny dream.
Was God there?

The jammed morning freeway leads to a redecision.
The parting clouds along the coastline reveal
The majesty of a glistening ocean caressing newly washed cliffs.
Was God there?

A stopped afternoon freeway provides another opportunity.
A twisting deserted mountain road through a magical forest
Accentuated by rain, mystified by fog.
Was God there?

Racing around curves, not in control, my body tenses.
Faith replaces anxiety and nature's magnificence fills me.
Hauntingly beautiful music enters and tears well.
Was God there?

You ask what I'm feeling and the dam overflows,
Let go of fear and hardness, stay open,
Go home and learn to meditate in Times Square.
Was God there?

I turn to look at you and
An iridescent rainbow frames a moon-faced Buddha.
I experience a new meaning of love.
Was God there?

At dusk, alone, I walk the beach, combing debris from the storm.
Two sparkling pieces of driftwood jump at me.
Each different, yet perfect for each of my teachers, each of my loves.
Was God there?

I am filled with peace.
God was here. God is here.

—Jordan Paul

Exercise 2A   Finding Your Higher Self

Recovering your memory, and therefore your ability to come from your Higher Self, begins with the identification of a particular time, place, and situation in which you felt truly fulfilled and at peace with yourself.

The following exercise will assist you in recovering your memory.

You will need a tape recorder for this exercise.

Part 1

Relax your body and your thoughts. Breathe deeply as you rest in a comfortable sitting position to allow yourself to open to your experience and your Higher Self. Continue this relaxation for one or two minutes before proceeding. If you have a favorite relaxation tape that you like to listen to, this is a good time to put it on for a few minutes.

Part 2

When you feel relaxed and open, answer the following question:

"What is the best example in my life of a time when I felt fulfilled, happy, and at peace with myself?"

Allow yourself to recall your best example, not necessarily a perfect example. Be specific about where you were, what you were doing, whom (if anyone) you were with and when it occurred.

Example: One day during the summer of 1982, I was walking on the beach with my five-year-old son in the late afternoon; we talked about how big the ocean was.

Allow yourself to re-create your special memory in your imagination. It may help to keep your eyes closed as you do this. Let yourself really feel and experience all the parts of that memory. What were you thinking? How did your body feel? What emotions did you have? What did you see? What did you hear? Allow yourself to be there once again, feeling fulfilled, happy, and at peace with yourself. Stay with this experience for at least one minute, savoring it, seeing, feeling, tasting, smelling, and hearing all that you can remember of those moments of your greatest fulfillment.

Part 3

Into your tape recorder speak the words and phrases that feel right in capturing your experience at that very special time. Take your time with this: you *will* be able to find the words that fit, that feel correct as you say them. As you speak, remain in touch with your memory of the experience, allowing your words to deepen the memory. You will soon begin to discover new depths, new dimensions of that time of fulfillment. Pause occasionally and use the quiet moments to go deeper into the experience, to remember more and more about it.

There will be a point when you feel complete, when you have described your experience of fulfillment as best you can. When you reach that point, pause.

Part 4

Ask yourself: "What is another example of a time when I experienced real fulfillment?" and repeat the process described in part 3, above.

Part 5

Repeat part 4 at least three times (or more if it feels right to you). Then stop, rewind the tape, and play it back. Know that you are beginning to hear the voice of your Higher Self. Listen deeply. While listening jot down in your notebook highlights of what you have said.

Part 6

Go back over your notes and listen again to the tape, looking for the patterns in what you experienced. What words or phrases capture or summarize the essentials of your experience of fulfillment? Write these words or phrases in your notebook.

Part 7

Once again, from a relaxed and open place, allow yourself to experience the essence of what you have identified as true fulfillment. As you experience that fulfillment here and now, know that you are operating from your Higher Self.

Recognize that this is what you say is true fulfillment for you and that it is what you are committed to. This commitment requires no effort and no further incentive. This is what your life is all about.

Part 8

If it feels right to you, proceed gently—and we emphasize *gently*—to think of a statement of your life purpose. Then take a few moments to write down this statement in your notebook. Keep it to ten to twenty words—the fewer the better. Remember, don't force this; if this is the right time for you, the words will come relatively easily. Otherwise, save this part of the exercise for another time. When your life purpose does emerge, it will become your personal affirmation, your personal prayer, the mantra from your Higher Self. The speaking of these sacred words are both a celebration of your Higher Self and a pathway back to that centered state.

Part 9

Now ask yourself the following questions:

1. How much of the time would I like to be operating in this state of fulfillment, in my Higher Self?

2. How often, up to this point in my life, have I experienced my Higher Self?

3. How often have I recognized the depth of my commitment to operating out of my Higher Self?

4. From now on, how much of the time am I committed to living in my Higher Self?

Know that your word is sacred. You are determining the quality of your life in each moment from now on.*

3. PERSONAL RESPONSIBILITY

In any conflict you have two levels of responsibility: (1) your part in setting up the conflict; and (2) how you react to the conflict.

You have a part in creating almost every unhappy situation in your life. So an important first step in finding the loving behavior is to discover your unloving behavior—how you set up the unhappy situation you are in. Of course, there are situations that you may not have created—being robbed, being hit by a car, experiencing the death of a loved one, and so on. But for these exercises, use situations in which you *definitely* had a part, such as your child lying to you, your girlfriend cheating on you, or an argument that occurred after you criticized your spouse, business partner, or parent.

There is no question about the other level of responsibility— that you are responsible for the way you react to any given situation. This is one of the most difficult things for people to accept. Since not everyone reacts the same way to the same circumstances, it is obvious that something inside each of us determines how we react. That something is our beliefs. We may not be able to change the actual situation, but we can change its effect on us.

As with everything else, you always have two choices: to react

*We give a special thanks and acknowledgment to Doug Kruschke, who created this exercise. Doug is president of In Synergy, a firm in Santa Monica, California, specializing in working with corporate executives who are seeking to integrate a large vision of their own and their employees' fulfillment with the continued success of their organizations.

protectively or to open and react lovingly.

Loving behavior is personally responsible behavior. To understand personal responsibility, it sometimes helps to start at the opposite end—victimhood.

Being a victim is certainly not taking responsibility or being loving, but there is a part of you that wants to be a victim. It's important not to deny that part but to acknowledge and accept it. One way to work with your victim feelings is to get into them as fully as possible, even to exaggerate them. You make yourself a victim when you believe there is no way you can make yourself happy. You feel helpless, stuck, waiting for another to change before you can be happy.

Exercise 3A   The Ways You Believe Yourself to Be a Victim

Here are a few examples of some typical victim statements:

- If the kids helped around the house, I wouldn't feel so hassled.
- If my spouse were less angry, I could open up.
- If my spouse listened to me, we could be close.
- If my spouse were more sexual, I could feel better about my body.
- It's men's fault that marriages fall apart.
- It's my parents' fault that I'm so resistant.
- It's my parents' fault that I'm so compliant.
- If I hadn't had such a rotten childhood, I wouldn't be so unhappy.
- If my father had been a better role model, I'd be more in touch with my emotions.
- If my boss were not so critical, I'd be more productive.

In your notebook; make a list of your own victim statements; and add to it whenever you come across new ones. When you set your mind to recognizing these beliefs, they will probably come up often.

Exercise 3B   Finding the Loving Response in a Conflict

This exercise, in two parts, is designed to put you in touch with your choices and their consequences. This is such an important concept that we have included much more discussion than in any other exercise. Please read the whole exercise, including the discussion, before doing either part 1 or 2.

Part 1   Taking Personal Responsibility for a Conflict

1.   When do you or did you feel like a victim?

(Preferably pick a situation you're still in. If you can't think of one, pick a past incident. This could be any conflict, especially those where you feel you are in a power struggle. Examples: your child has been lying to you; your mate isn't interested in being sexual with you; you've caught your mate cheating on you; you have an employee who's not performing up to his/her previous standards.)

2.   How are you responsible for causing the initial incident?

3.   Describe your behavior in the conflict. How are you responsible for creating the interaction and the consequences?

EXAMPLE: I walked in on my girlfriend while she was in bed with another man. I guess my responsibility was that I didn't call first, and also there must have been something going on between us that led her to do that and not to tell me about it, but I'm not sure what that was. It's hard for me to know how I was responsible for causing the initial incident. Maybe I wasn't totally honest.

What followed was awful. We had a big fight. I don't think I've ever been so angry. I still remember shaking with fear and anger. I finally left, telling her I never wanted to see her again. I went home feeling self-righteous but very alone. We did get back together, but it was never the same. I guess she felt attacked by my anger and blame and she got very defensive. I was just as much part of the insults and threats that followed as she was.

Part 2   Finding the Loving Response in a Conflict

4.   Using the situation you described in part 1, think about what you could have done or could do now that would be loving, and complete the following statement: "A reaction that is loving and personally responsible is . . . "

EXAMPLE: Instead of getting angry, I could have then or could now want to learn about my part in creating this situation. Had I given the message that I would not tolerate that kind of behavior, thereby setting up a situation where she might go behind my back? Were there things going on between us that we had not confronted?

I could learn about why I get angry and the consequences of that behavior. I could care enough to be concerned about her. I could learn about the very good reasons she must have had for behaving as she did, both in sleeping with the other man and in the interactions that followed. I could explore and learn about my expectations and beliefs about sexual fidelity and about relationships.

Does this sound difficult to do? You're right, it is. We never said loving behavior was going to be easy. The "format for learning" exercises in chapter 4 will help you expand your understanding of your current behavior and create behavior that is more loving.

A good place to start now, however, is to remember that *the intention to learn will always be loving*. To want to learn about yourself and to want to understand the very good reasons the other person has for his/her behavior is loving in itself and will lead to other loving behaviors.

Don't mistake a loving response with giving yourself up. That's never loving, nor is taking responsibility for others—that is, doing for others what they can do for themselves, or trying to "fix" them, or offering them awarenesses that they haven't asked for or don't want. When you take responsibility for another's exploration, you may be avoiding your own.

Discussion from the Workshop

SHARING: I'm having trouble with this. Say you're trying to learn about somebody. You have all the best intentions to understand her, but she sticks with her position. Then you're in an argument situation with both sides trying to explain how they feel and neither side believing the other and you're both trying to learn. Then what?

MARGIE: You're not trying to learn. Explanations are not the intention to learn. That is what is subtle about this. Often you think you want to learn, but if you're explaining—if you have to be right, to win, to have your way—there is no intention to learn.

SHARING: What if you don't need to be right, but just don't want to be criticized?

MARGIE: If the need to protect yourself against criticism is the most important thing, then you are still closed to learning. You have to be willing to be criticized. In order to learn, you have to be willing to have all the bad things happen that you are afraid of: being criticized, blamed, or seen in the wrong, or being seen in some other way you don't want to be seen. That is why it's so hard.

SHARING: When you have accepted the criticism and considered whether you can learn something from it, and you're open to experiencing whatever pain is involved, then what do you do?

MARGIE: If somebody is intent on criticizing you and is not open to learning about why *she* needs to do that, then you need to find the loving action you should take for yourself. For me, being with someone whose sole intent is to criticize me is not a loving thing. So, one loving response would be to say "When you want to talk openly and explore, let's do that. But if all you want to do is criticize me, then I don't want to be around you." I have found that for me, the loving behavior is simply not to be around somebody who is critical. I don't like it.

JORDAN: I agree: it is not loving to yourself to stay in a situation where the other person's intent is only to criticize you.

Of course you might stay just long enough to learn something about yourself. What's your part in the difficulty? If there is any validity to the criticism, you can learn from that. Do you take criticism personally and feel wrong and/or responsible when another person is upset? When you don't take criticism personally, you understand that whenever a person is judgmental, he or she is off center. But in a situation where essentially you are being beaten up emotionally, it's best to leave.

Most of us don't even recognize that we have the option to leave. This comes from childhood, when leaving the room in an emotionally or physically painful situation would have caused even more pain, so we had to stay and take it. As adults, we often act like five-year-olds; not knowing that we do indeed have the right to leave any situation in which we are being abused. You do not have to "take it," and you don't need to get the other person to stop. That's an attempt to outcontrol her, and then you are in a power struggle. That may be what you need to learn.

So, if you're not going to attempt to control the other person, the loving option is to leave for a while. And that's hard to do. Very often, people don't leave until they get angry. They have to wait until they can justify such drastic action and then they leave blaming the other person for their anger. That is another protection. The loving behavior is to know that you always have the right to leave, to say without anger, "I don't like this; this does not feel good. If you want to learn—if you want to learn together—I'd like to do that, and I'll come back later. But if you want to go through this same kind of interaction again, I'll leave again." Taking care of yourself with anger is an ego behavior. Taking care of yourself without blame is the behavior that will leave you feeling balanced and best about yourself. This is not easily done. So, as always,

70

whenever you get hooked, you have opportunity to learn about the self-limiting beliefs that are creating your unloving behavior.

MARGIE: So when people say things like, "You're hurting me" as a criticism, they're not open to learning about their hurt, they just want to make someone else wrong. They're blaming another for their feelings. They're not recognizing that feelings are very important to learn from, that they're a key, a sign saying, "Look inside! There's a belief here. There's something to learn here." You can learn about that feeling's underlying beliefs, where the feeling comes from, and what it's about by asking, "What is my lesson here? What do I need to learn?"

When the other person's intent is to learn about her feelings, it is loving to help her. If she wants help, she'll ask for it: "Would you help me to learn about this feeling I'm having?" But if she's only saying, "I want to tell you my feelings," she is not open to learning and she's not enlisting your help in becoming open; she just wants to have control over you. So, being a part of that is not loving.

If somebody says, "You're hurting my feelings," a loving response is always to look at yourself to see what your intention is. In addition, a loving response would be to say, "Why do you believe that? What would I want to do that for? And why do you believe that it's possible for me to do that to you?" If she is willing to look at that, if she is willing to move into the intention to learn, then it would be loving to be there to help her. But if she just says, "Because you are. You're hurting my feelings because you're never around. You're hurting my feelings because . . . " then there is no point in the interaction. At that point, a loving response would be, "I don't like being blamed for what you're feeling. When you're willing to explore, let me know.''

SHARING: In your system, can one do whatever one wants? A friend of mine did *est* and then just went crazy—had affairs, left her husband—and I think that's wrong.

JORDAN: You're feeling very judgmental about her behavior and that blocks your learning. So try to look at this with an intention to learn—to learn about her reasons for behaving as she did and about your judgmental reaction.

As with all behavior, there are always important reasons behind someone's choice to have an affair. For your friend, it may have been a protection. Or perhaps she's addicted to sex—addicted to the affirmation that she gets from sex. Maybe it was her way of running away from intimacy with her husband. There are all kinds of unhealthy reasons why a person would choose to have affairs. But to the person making the choice, they are important reasons, and that choice probably appeared to be the best thing your friend could do at the time. But there's always another choice. She could choose to learn about her part in the situation, her fears and beliefs, and why her husband does what he does, and whether her husband is open to explore that with her. There are a lot of things she could learn before leaving her marriage. A person's first reaction is often, ''Well, I could leave or I could accept the situation the way it is.'' The option rarely considered is: ''I could explore and learn a lot about this upsetting situation.'' She may eventually leave the marriage—that might turn out to be the most loving thing to do—but people usually leave prematurely, before they learn anything about their part in the problems. Then, they usually go right into other relationships with different people but with the same dynamics.

Since the woman you described isn't here, would you like to explore why you're being judgmental of your friend's behavior?

(In the interaction that followed, this woman explored her pain over an infidelity in her past, her fears concerning her husband's love for her, and her desire to have control over other people's actions. She saw her judgments as a protection—a way of directing the focus away from her own painful feelings—and recognized the devastating effect these repressed emotions were having on her relationships.)

SHARING: How do you not take personally another person's negative behavior toward you?

MARGIE: When you take another person's protective behavior personally, you feel attacked and you can't be there for that person in a loving way. If you see that the person is fearful and know that a protection is always a cry for help, and if you could respond from love, you could be soft, open, and interested. You wouldn't take that person's unloving behavior as an affront to you. Therefore, you would not be in pain, and so, rather than reacting defensively, you could reach out in real concern. You could feel forgiveness, in the truest sense of the word, from your Higher Self, not from your judgmental ego.

JORDAN: In the past, when Margie got irritated with me, my first reaction was always to tighten up and get defensive: "You're not going to do that to me! I'll give it right back to you!" But I found that if I didn't take her irritation personally—if I didn't feel like a bad boy, if I didn't feel wrong—then I could realize that she's hurting when she's irritated, and I could react in an entirely different way. I could be caring in the face of her

JORDAN   unloving behavior, rather than see it as an assault on me
(cont.):   and then become protected.

The steps for this exercise are amplified in the exercise below. Now complete the exercise.

1. When do you or did you feel like a victim?
    (Preferably pick a situation you're still in. If you can't think of one, pick a past incident.)

2. How are you responsible for causing the initial incident?

3. Describe your behavior in the conflict. How are you responsible for creating the interaction and the consequences?

4. Using the situation you described in part 1, think about what you could have done or could now do that would be loving and complete the following statement: "A reaction that is loving and personally responsible is . . . "

Exercise 3C   Checklist—Self-limiting Beliefs about Responsibility

____ 1.   I can't make myself happy if someone around me is protecting him/herself.

____ 2.   I should never do anything that upsets or hurts another's feelings.

____ 3.   Others should never do anything that hurts or upsets me.

____ 4.   I don't need anybody.

____ 5.   Other people can make me happy.

____ 6.   Other people can make me unhappy.

____ 7.   I can't take care of myself.

____ 8.   I can't be alone. I'll die if I'm alone.

____ 9.   When I'm hurt, it's someone else's fault.

____ 10.   I shouldn't feel happy when people around me are unhappy.

____ 11.   I shouldn't do something that makes me happy if it upsets someone else.

____ 12.   I can make someone else be open and loving.

____ 13.   I can get other people to stop their protected behavior.

____ 14.   It's up to me to make the people I care about happy.

____ 15.   When I'm unhappy, it's someone else's fault.

____ 16.   When others around me are unhappy, it's my fault.

____ 17.   It's my responsibility to make sure that the people around me don't fail.

___ 18. If I don't take responsibility for other people's happiness and unhappiness, I'm not a caring person.

___ 19. I don't deserve to make myself happy. Therefore, someone else has to take responsibility for telling me it's okay to do what makes me happy.

___ 20. If I take responsibility for my happiness, I'm being selfish.

___ 21. It's selfish of me to be happy unless everyone around me is happy.

___ 22. (For women) As a woman, it's my job to see that everyone is happy.

___ 22. (For men) As a man, it's my job to make sure that the woman in my life is taken care of financially.

___ 23. It's up to other people to make me feel good about myself by approving of me.

___ 24. I'm not responsible for my feelings. Other people make me feel happy, sad, angry, frustrated, shut down, or depressed.

___ 25. I'm not responsible for my behavior. Other people make me yell, act crazy, get sick, laugh, cry, get violent, leave, or fail.

___ 26. If other people are angry at me, I made them feel that way and I'm responsible for fixing their feelings.

___ 27. If I'm angry, someone else made me feel that way, and that person is responsible for fixing my feelings.

___ 28. I'm responsible for meeting my partner's sexual needs.

___ 29. My partner is responsible for meeting my sexual needs.

___ 30. If I'm loving and I make myself happy, the other person will take advantage of me.

___ 31. If I'm loving, the other person will never change and be the way I want him/her to be.

___ 32. If I'm loving and I take responsibility for my happiness, I won't need a relationship.

___ 33. If I'm in a relationship, the happier and more loving I become, the further apart we will get because I won't need a relationship.

___ 34. It's my parents' fault, or my partner's fault, or someone else's fault, that:
    ___ I'm unloving.
    ___ I'm scared to be alone.
    ___ I don't believe relationships can work.
    ___ I'm so screwed up.
    ___ I can't change.
    ___ I can't take care of myself.
    ___ I'm in a job I hate.
    ___ I'm an alcoholic, drug addict, compulsive overeater, or workaholic.

4. UNMET EXPECTATIONS

We all have expectations. They are those statements that often start with, "If you really loved me . . . ." Many have said that, ideally, we should live without expectations, since this would keep us totally in the present moment. Obviously, this is unrealistic.

We suggest a more practical approach. Accept that you're going to have expectations, but when your expectations aren't met, know that you have two choices:

1. To protect by blaming. When you blame others for making you unhappy because they have failed to meet your expectations, you are accusing them of being unloving. They will probably get defensive and begin trying to prove that they do care. Then you will have arguments over whether they care, or not. Because of your belief, they'll never convince you, and everyone will wind up feeling uncared for and misunderstood.

2. To be loving by taking personal responsibility. When you learn from your unhappiness, you can discover the following: whether your expectations do in fact have anything to do with caring about others; what you do to create and perpetuate your unhappiness; how to take responsibility for doing what's necessary to change your present unhappiness.

Anytime you find yourself being judgmental, look for the expectation that wasn't met and then look for the belief that underlies the expectation.

Exercise 4A   Learning from Unmet Expectations

Think of a recent time when your expectations weren't met.

1. Describe the incident, your reaction to it, the other person's reaction to your behavior, and the scenario that followed.

2. Rewrite the scenario with the intention to learn. (An important aspect of this will be to discover whether what you have believed to be caring fits the definition of loving behavior.)

3. Go to the other person with an intention to learn. (You will now have the opportunity to learn about caring on a deeper level.)

Exercise 4B Checklist—Self-limiting Beliefs about Expectations

If you really loved me (cared about me), you would . . . :

or:

If I were really important to you, you would . . . :

____ 1. Never do anything that upsets me.

____ 2. Remember my birthday (or anniversary).

____ 3. Never be late.

____ 4. Call me when you're going to be late.

____ 5. Be turned on to me.

____ 6. Make love to me whenever I want you to.

____ 7. Never want to do anything without me.

____ 8. Never walk away when I'm talking.

____ 9. Stop reading when I walk in the room.

____ 10. Watch TV with me.

____ 11. Always want to do what I want.

____ 12. Agree with me.

____ 13. Have the same interests I do.

____ 14. Lose weight (or gain weight).

____ 15. Make more money.

____ 16. Spend less money.

____ 17. Keep the house clean.

____ 18. Do the dishes.

____ 19. Eat right.

____ 20. Take your vitamins.

____ 21. Dress the way I want you to.

____ 22. Be affectionate.

____ 23. Be affectionate in public.

____ 24. Put your clothes away.

____ 25. Share the responsibilities at home.

____ 26. Always have an orgasm.

____ 27. Enjoy all the kinds of foreplay and sexual activities that I enjoy.

____ 28. Not have an orgasm until I do.

____ 29. Wash your genitals before coming to bed.

____ 30. Make me happy.

____ 31. Never take vacations without me.

____ 32. Take care of me.

____ 33. Always have dinner ready when I want it.

____ 34. Always look nice.

____ 35. Read my mind.

____ 36. Anticipate my needs.

____ 37. Never let me oversleep.

____ 38. Never be attracted to anyone else.

____ 39. Never make love to anyone else.

____ 40. Make my needs more important than your own.

____ 41. Give in to me.

____ 42. Do things my way.

____ 43. Call me every day.

____ 44. Make up first.

____ 45. Never argue with me.

____ 46. Buy me expensive presents.

____ 47. Give me more money.

____ 48. Solve my problems for me.

____ 49. Do all the things that I don't like to do.

____ 50. Make me feel good about myself.

____ 51. Take care of me whenever I'm sick.

____ 52. Not have outside interests or hobbies.

____ 53. Always want to be with me.

____ 54. Stop drinking or taking drugs.

____ 55. Come home earlier from work.

____ 56. Spend more time with the kids.

____ 57. Stop watching so much TV.

___ 58. Go to bed at the same time I do.

___ 59. Take a shower every day.

___ 60. Never lie to me.

___ 61. Never think of old lovers.

___ 62. Make my unhappiness go away.

___ 63. Stop being friends with old lovers.

___ 64. Stop being friends with people I don't like.

___ 65. Tear up old love letters.

___ 66. Be excited about the things that excite me.

___ 67. Be interested in my problems.

___ 68. Make everything right for me.

___ 69. Love my pets.

___ 70. Love my parents.

___ 71. Love my children, be good to my children.

___ 72. Get rid of everything that is a reminder of your previous marriages.

___ 73. Be serious when I want to be serious.

___ 74. Be miserable when I'm miserable.

___ 75. Be happy when I'm happy.

___ 76. Be miserable when I'm away.

Exercise 4C   Checklist—Self-limiting Beliefs about Expectations for Children

If you really loved me (cared about me), you would . . .

or:

If I were really important to you, you would . . . :

___ 1.   Never do anything that upsets me.

___ 2.   Agree with me.

___ 3.   Lose weight (or gain weight).

___ 4.   Go to college.

___ 5.   Do your homework.

___ 6.   Get good grades.

___ 7.   Eat what I cook.

___ 8. Eat with the family.

___ 9. Finish everything on your plate.

___ 10. Keep your room clean.

___ 11. Do your chores.

___ 12. Eat right.

___ 13. Take your vitamins.

___ 14. Dress the way I want you to.

___ 15. Be affectionate.

___ 16. Put your clothes away.

___ 17. Give in to me.

___ 18. Do things my way.

___ 19. Call me when you're going to be late.

___ 20. Take a shower every day.

___ 21. Stop watching so much TV.

___ 22. Stop taking drugs.

___ 23. Never argue with me.

___ 24. Talk to me about your problems.

___ 25. Never lie to me.

___ 26. Stop being friends with kids I don't like.

___ 27. Become a doctor (or a lawyer, etc.).

___ 28. Not leave dirty dishes around.

___ 29. Have good manners.

___ 30. Say "please" and "thank you."

___ 31. Be good in front of my friends.

___ 32. Appreciate the things I buy for you.

___ 33. Be the person I want to be.

5. REVIEWING THE DAY FOR LOVING AND UNLOVING BEHAVIOR

It helps to review your loving and unloving behavior on a daily basis. You can do this aloud with a partner or just think about it before going to sleep at night. It is also a wonderful thing to do with the entire family, perhaps at the dinner table.

Each day, think of one or two unloving things you did during the day. Focus on how each behavior was unloving toward yourself, how it didn't leave you feeling good about yourself. In the midst of a conflict, did you try to control another person, or did you give in, shut down, or become indifferent? Recapture how you felt about yourself. What would have been loving behavior? What fears and beliefs got in the way of your behaving in that way?

Now think of one or two loving things you did. Recapture how you felt when behaving that way. Allow yourself to drift into sleep with the images and feelings of being your Higher Self.

A caution is in order at this point: Do not expect your learnings to be accomplished easily. You are just beginning your journey down a very unusual road.

It is the courage to be open and loving which is the manifestation of underlying strength and power. And it is only in embracing the possibility that you have a Higher Self that knows how to love, that knows the truth within, that is truly powerful, that you can begin to face and dismantle the false beliefs of the protected self, the ego. You can't begin to look at these and deal with them if you don't believe there's anything else. You can never move into the feeling of personal power unless you recognize truly that there's a peaceful place within you that is already there, that doesn't have to be developed and doesn't have to be fixed.

—Jordan and Margaret Paul,
from *If You Really Loved Me*

· 4 ·

BASIC LEARNING SKILLS

The following exercises and formats will help you focus your learning. They will guide you into many different areas and give you a fuller picture of why things are the way they are in your life. *This includes the critical area of your willingness to learn.*

In this chapter, you may work individually or with a partner. Alone, either write out your answers or speak them into a tape recorder—whichever is most helpful in bringing you to your answers. Working with another person will be an entirely different experience. Your partner can help you focus and perhaps go deeper than you can go alone. On the other hand, it is often tempting for your partner to try to influence you; or it may be easier for you to slip into focusing on the other person rather than on yourself. See what works best for you. No matter what happens, you can learn from it.

This chapter contains the basic formats for learning. All of the Self-limiting Beliefs checklists can be used with all of the formats in this chapter. You can start using the formats right away even though many questions within them are the subject of later chapters. As you do the exercises in those chapters, redoing these formats will increase the depth of your learning.

Discussion from the Workshop

SHARING: I've done this workshop twice before and this is the first time I've understood that the real key is challenging the beliefs. That's how I get rid of the old baggage. If I don't do that, I just don't achieve anything. But what if you want to challenge a belief but you don't have the confidence to do it?

MARGIE: If you really want to challenge a belief, then you go ahead and challenge it no matter how frightened you are. Challenging a belief is frightening—there's no way around that. But sometimes we just have to act. You know, we are all terrified that bad things are going to happen. You just have to tell yourself, "Okay, I'm willing to fail," or, "I'm willing to lose," or, "I'm willing to be laughed at," or whatever it is you're afraid of. You have to be willing to have the worst thing happen. This the only way through the fear.

You are also dealing with your ego here. Your ego wants to prove that it's right. When you challenge your ego, you're trying to prevent it from sabotaging your efforts. Your ego always wants its own beliefs to rule.

But you also have a will. *You* decide. You can hear the voice of the ego, and you can hear the voice of the Higher Self. The voice of the ego is very loud and the voice of the Higher Self is very soft, but you can hear it if you want to. It is your choice which one you listen to.

When you decide to challenge your beliefs, that ego is going to come in powerfully: "What are you, nuts? How can you do this? You're going to die. You're going to lose everything." It's your choice to listen to the old beliefs or to go ahead without them.

SHARING: So, we are learning to silence the ego.

MARGIE: Yes, and the only way you can do that is by challenging its beliefs. Once you see that a belief is false, the ego can no longer hit you with it. You must thus quiet the ego and listen carefully to hear your Higher Self.

6. LEARNING FROM A CONFLICT

Learning from a conflict is the essential goal. This is the basic format you will be returning to over and over.

Exercise 6A   Basic Format for Learning from a Conflict

1. What is the situation I am unhappy or upset about?

2. How am I protecting in this situation right now? (See chapter 5 for details.)

3. What do I hope will happen as a result of my reacting in this way?

4. Are my protections working to get me what I want?

5. What are the actual results (consequences), for my relationship and for myself, of my reacting protectively? (See chapter 6.)

6. What is my part in creating the situation? In what ways have I been protecting myself in the events leading up to this conflict? (See chapter 6.)

(If you have difficulty answering this question, ask the person with whom you are in conflict.)

7. What fears/beliefs (about protections, about my adequacy, and about expectations) are creating my protective behavior? (See chapter 7.)

8. What in my past experiences created these fears/beliefs?

9. What would be the loving behavior? What would be the opposite of how I've been protecting? What would be the behavior that would bring me joy, support my growth, enhance my self-esteem, and make me happy as well as support the other person's growth? Describe how the behavior looks. Be concrete. (Review chapter 3.)

10. If I can't do that, what fears/beliefs are getting in the way of my behaving in a loving way? (See chapter 7.)

11. Am I willing to challenge the accuracy of these fears/beliefs with loving behavior? (If not, you have chosen to stay stuck with your unhappiness. To get unstuck, answer the following: What purpose is being served by my hanging on to this belief and what am I afraid would happen if I let go of this belief?)

Once you have learned more about your protections and you understand them in depth you can go directly to questions 7 through 11 in any conflict. This format can be used over and over again.

7. CHALLENGING SELF-LIMITING BELIEFS

Challenging beliefs is a simple yet difficult process. It is the heart of the transformational process. Use this format to learn about every self-limiting belief you have.

Here are some of the most common self-limiting beliefs.

Beliefs about control:
- Attempting to control others through guilt and fear, by using my anger, blame, judgments, or cries of "poor me," will eventually get me what I want.
- Attempting to control another person is justifiable if he/she does something I feel is wrong.
- In a relationship, if I'm not in control, then I'll be controlled.
- I can get another person out of his/her protected behavior.

Beliefs about compliance:
- If I do things to make myself happy, I'm selfish. To be unselfish, I have to give myself up to make others happy.
- I have to give myself up to make the other person happy, or that person won't love me.
- Going along with what others want, even if it's not what I want, is a loving behavior.
- What I feel and want isn't important.
- I should never do anything that upsets another person or hurts another person's feelings.

Beliefs about resistance:
- Rebelling is a good way to establish one's independent identity.
- It's the controlling person's fault that I resist or rebel.
- If I don't rebel, I'll be controlled.

Beliefs about indifference:
- I can avoid problems by becoming indifferent.

- It's better to shut down and withdraw than to reach out and risk rejection.

Beliefs about adequacy:
- I'm not good enough. Therefore, I have to
  — control to get what I want.
  — give in to avoid rejection.
  — shut down to avoid the pain that I can't handle.

- I'm inadequate, unlovable, not good enough because . . . .
- If I'm wrong about anything, it means I'm stupid or not okay and I'll be rejected.
- I can't handle pain, especially the pain of rejection.

Beliefs about expectations:
- If I were really important to you (or if you really loved me or cared about me) you would . . . .

Exercise 7A Basic Format for Challenging Self-limiting Beliefs

1. Where did I get this belief? What were the circumstances in which I first remember accepting this belief?

2. How does this belief affect my life right now? What are the situations in which this belief comes up?

3. What are the negative consequences of this belief?

4. What are the positive consequences of continuing this belief? (What am I getting? What am I avoiding?)

5. What is the behavior that would challenge this belief? (If I didn't believe this, if I began to call this belief a lie, how would I feel and behave?)

6. Am I willing to try out that new behavior? (If not, you need more time, more information, and/or more negative consequences.)

8. EXPLORING BELIEFS ABOUT RIGHT AND WRONG

Following is a partial list of conflict issues. These are the areas in which you may have strong beliefs about what is right and what is wrong.

> Sex (frequency, technique, initiation of)
> Money (control of, uptightness about, looseness with)
> Politics
> Religion
> In-laws (attitude toward, reactions to)
> Communications (amount of, clarity of)
> Commitments
> Responsibilities
> Holidays and gift-giving
> Criticalness
> Manners (table manners, social etiquette)
> Television
> Sports
> Schoolwork (grades, homework)

Children (how to raise, how many, when, whether to have any)

Other relationships (sexual and nonsexual)

Looks (grooming, weight, dress, neatness, cleanliness)

Housekeeping (neatness, chores, who does what)

Time (compulsive about punctuality, always late)

Time (how time is spent, amount of time spent together)

Vacations (how often, how spent)

Work (differing attitudes, priority in life)

Use of substances (alcohol, drugs, tobacco)

Health (exercising too much or too little, taking care of self physically)

Food (what is healthy, amounts, who cooks, when to eat)

Language (proper use, choice of words)

Humor (lack of, being put down by)

Affection (amount, how expressed)

Pets (whose responsibility, whether to have)

Exploring these issues of right versus wrong is an important part of your learning. The following format will take you not only into your beliefs but into your need to be in control. This need to be right and impose your beliefs on others is a very basic issue for everyone.

Exercise 8A Basic Format for Exploring Beliefs about Right and Wrong

Answer the following questions, using the issues listed on page 90 or any other issues about which you are in conflict.

1. What do I believe is right or wrong and how is this belief being "violated"?

2. Why do I believe this?

3. What purpose does it serve for me to hold on to this belief?

4. What am I afraid would happen if I let go of this belief?

5. Is this a universal belief, shared by everyone throughout the world?
(If your answer is yes, you might do some research to see if it really is. If your answer is no, go on to the next question.)

6. Why is it so important to me to have my way on this issue?

7. How do I make others wrong when they don't believe as I do or don't do things my way?

8. What am I afraid would happen if I didn't make others wrong?

9. What do I hope will happen by making others wrong?

10. What happens when I attempt to impose my beliefs on others?

11. Why is it so important that others believe the same as I do?

12. Am I willing to test the accuracy of my beliefs? If yes, how am I going to do that? If no, why not?

9. LEARNING FROM YOUR FEELINGS

Most people have no idea what is causing their feelings. Protective feelings always come from beliefs. When you accept that, you take full charge of and responsibility for your feelings. Protective feelings will never be changed by trying to change them. They will change only when your beliefs change.

You don't choose to feel depressed, angry, or scared, but you have chosen the beliefs that create these feelings. You can avoid taking responsibility for your feelings by believing that others cause your feelings or that feelings just descend on you and you are powerless to do anything about it. Taking responsibility for your beliefs and feelings is one of the most loving things you can do.

"Taking responsibility for your feelings" doesn't mean blaming yourself, hating yourself, feeling guilty, or emotionally beating yourself for all the mistakes you've made. The idea is not to stop blaming somebody else only to turn all of your judgments against yourself. The idea is to love others and yourself—remembering that you have good reasons for your behavior, looking for and understanding the beliefs that create your behavior, accepting and forgiving, and then finding the new, more loving beliefs on which to base your new, more loving behavior. The last step of the cycle occurs when you finally test the new beliefs and behaviors to see how they work.

One of the hardest truths to accept is that it is not possible to be emotionally hurt by another person. Since feelings are a result of beliefs, if you are feeling emotionally hurt, *it is because of your beliefs, not someone else's actions.*

Not taking another's behavior personally is the goal. Once you have corrected your erroneous beliefs, your behavior will look and feel entirely different to other people. You will see and feel things from a new perspective, so you can then behave with caring toward yourself and others. You will see that others are creating pain for themselves, and if they choose not to change their unloving behavior, then you will know that the behavior that is loving to yourself is to get away from them.

Exercise 9A   Basic Format for Learning from Your Feelings

1. How am I feeling right now? (Write down as many feelings as you are aware of:)

Angry	Threatened	Hurt	Guilty
Irritated	Insecure	Disappointed	Unworthy
Frustrated	Jealous	Depressed/"dead"	Wrong
Scared	Blaming/victimized	Unlovable	Inadequate
Uptight	Resentful	Anxious	Bored

2. Where in my body do I feel these?

3. How deeply am I allowing myself to feel these feelings?

*4. What are the judgments I have about feeling this way? Do I feel wrong, guilty, inadequate, unlovable, weak, stupid?

*5. What do I fear would happen if I just allowed myself to reach the depths of these feelings?

6. What events from my past are connected to these feelings? What circumstances from the past do these feelings remind me of?

7. Am I interpreting another person's behavior as an assault on me?

*8. How am I hoping another person will respond? Do I want him/her to do something? What am I hoping he/she will do about my feelings?

9. If my feelings are blaming—resentment, anger, having been wronged, hurt, "poor me," righteousness—what vulnerable feelings are being covered up? Sadness, fear, loneliness, disconnectedness, uncertainty, confusion?

10. What are the beliefs that are creating both my vulnerable feelings and my blaming feelings?

11. What happens in my relationship(s) when I protect against my vulnerable feelings?

12. What would be the loving behavior toward myself that would lead to my feeling better?

13. What fears/beliefs are getting in the way of my loving behavior?

10. LEARNING FROM YOUR REACTION TO AN EMOTIONAL VIOLATION

Personal violations occur more frequently than we would care to believe. Violations are usually thought of only on their most physically violent level, like rape or beating. But violation occurs whenever something is done to someone that he or she doesn't want done. In this light, violation takes on a whole new meaning and significance in our lives both as violators and as the ones being violated.

Violation is a hard word for most of us to hear. We don't want to think of ourselves as violating others, nor do we want to look at how often we have been violated. Without conscious intent to hurt others, violations occur even in the most loving relationships. We all do it, and it's important to not blame ourselves or others. We aren't bad people, but violate out of fear and ignorance.

Because more subtle violations are usually not understood as such, children can be violated over and over again by even the most loving parents. We all have the basic right to not have anything done to our bodies that we don't want, including hitting or pinching and

---

*The answers to questions 4, 5, and 8 relate to self-limiting beliefs and can be explored separately for deeper learning.

even demonstrations of affection like touching or kissing. Emotional violations include any disregard for our right to think, feel, and be who we are.

When our personhood is continually violated we not only do not learn to know and respect our own boundaries, but we don't learn to respect the boundaries of others. So we allow ourselves to be violated, not even knowing that we have the right to not allow it. And, of course, we violate others, usually without conscious awareness, remaining puzzled why people don't feel cared about and like being with us.

The following checklists will make you more aware of violations. Learning about how you violate others is linked to becoming tuned in to how you are violated, so the checklists are followed by an exercise for learning from the times when you are emotionally or physically violated.

Exercise 10A   Checklist—Ways You May Be Violating Another's Boundaries

Physical Violations
___ 1.   Beating, hitting, slapping, spanking.
___ 2.   Standing threateningly close, making threatening gestures.
___ 3.   Holding another person against that person's will.
___ 4.   Pinching or squeezing any part of another person's body.
___ 5.   Touching, tickling, or kissing that is uninvited or unwanted.
___ 6.   Manipulating, forcing sex.
List other ways you violate other people's physical boundaries.

Emotional Violations
___ 1.   Snooping:
　　　　—Listening in on private conversations.
　　　　—Reading another's mail or personal writing, looking through
　　　　　another person's personal belongings.
___ 2.   Lying.
___ 3.   Revealing personal information about a person that he or she doesn't want
　　　　known.

95

___ 4. Intruding on another person's important private time.

___ 5. Manipulating another person through some form of control—anger, threats, insults, tears, complaints, withdrawal and many others—instilling guilt or fear, making another wrong in order to get that person to:
>   —spend time with you.
>   —have sex with you.
>   —support your addiction to alcohol or drugs, etc.
>   —agree with your point of view.
>   —spend his or her time in a specific way.

___ 6. Discounting another person's feelings of being violated.

List other ways you violate other people's emotional boundaries.

Exercise 10B   Checklist—Ways You May Be Allowing Others to Violate Your Boundaries

___ 1. Feeling guilty/wrong when you do something to make yourself happy and the other person is angry, blaming and/or telling you that you are selfish.

___ 2. Staying around someone who is attempting to make you feel guilty or afraid.

___ 3. Staying around someone who is threatening you physically or actually harming you physically.

___ 4. Allowing someone to touch you, kiss you, or have sex with you when it is not what you want.

___ 5. Ignoring your sense that someone is lying to you.

___ 6. Spending time with someone when you don't want to.

___ 7. Agreeing to do things you don't want to do.

___ 8. Agreeing with someone when it means denying your own beliefs, point of view, or inner knowing.

Exercise 10C   Basic Format for Learning from Your Reaction to an Emotional Violation

When you have been emotionally violated in any way, your reaction will determine how you feel about yourself. Your buttons get pushed whenever another person criticizes you, belittles you, is angry with you, or demonstrates any other abusive behavior. Whenever you take another's behavior personally, it's because it taps into your own self-doubt. That's your opportunity to learn about your self-doubt and begin to clear it out. Following is the format you can use.

1. What do I feel when I am violated emotionally (criticized, made the butt of a joke or sarcasm, ignored, discounted, teased, made wrong, belittled)? E.g., hurt, angry, abused, used, uncared for, indignant.

2. What happens in my body? Do I feel a knot in my stomach, queasy, weak, deadened, tense, pain in various parts of my body, faint?

3. How do I react when I feel I have been emotionally violated?
   Attack back, wimp out, smile, withdraw, get embarrassed, try to be different to please the other person, go along with the "humor," inform the other that my feelings are hurt and I'm not going to take it anymore, blame myself, make nice?

4. What is my part in this emotional violation? What set me up to be vulnerable to it? What expectations or "needs" of mine weren't met?

5. Why am I taking this personally? Do my hurt feelings serve some purpose? What are they protecting me from?

6. What happens to the relationship as a consequence of my reactions?

7. What is the loving thing to do—the behavior that will enhance my self-esteem?

8. What fears/beliefs are getting in the way of my loving behavior?

11. QUESTIONS TO ASK WHEN WANTING TO LEARN ABOUT ANOTHER PERSON

As with everything else, the results of using this format will depend on your intention, since that is what determines the outcome of any interaction.

   If you intend to learn about another and you say gently and lovingly, "You know, what you've done is upsetting me, but I know you must have some important reasons for it. Would you tell me what they are?"—the other person will probably perceive that you really want to know. But if you say accusingly and judgmentally, "You know, what you've done is really upsetting me, and I know you must have some important reasons for it. I'd like to know what they are," there is no intent to learn on your part, and the other person will immediately know that you really want only to accuse. The words don't give the message. The questions listed below are offered only as suggestions. Bear in mind, however, that our intention comes through in the tone of voice and in the energy that we put out, and those are the things that will be responded to. Everyone senses consciously or unconsciously, whether another person is open or upset, shut down or judgmental.

- What you've done is upsetting to me, but I know you must have some important reasons for it. Would you tell me what they are?
- You seem upset (or angry, distant, defensive, etc.). Have I done something that hurt you?
- Is there something I'm doing that's upsetting to you?

Once you are clear about the conflict or the upsetting feelings, then one or both of you can move to the appropriate format for exploration.

SYMPTOMS OF INNER PEACE

Be on the lookout for symptoms of inner peace. The hearts of a great many have already been exposed to inner peace and it is possible that people everywhere could come down with it in epidemic proportions. This could pose a serious threat to what has, up to now, been a fairly stable condition of conflict in the world.

Some signs and symptoms of inner peace:

— *A tendency to think and act spontaneously rather than on fears based on past experiences.*
— *An unmistakable ability to enjoy each moment.*
— *A loss of interest in judging other people.*
— *A loss of interest in interpreting the actions of others.*
— *A loss of interest in conflict.*
— *A loss of the ability to worry. (This is a very serious symptom.)*
— *Frequent, overwhelming episodes of appreciation.*
— *Contented feelings of connectedness with others and nature.*
— *An increasing tendency to let things happen rather than make them happen.*
— *An increased susceptibility to the love extended by others as well as the uncontrollable urge to extend it.*

WARNING!

If you have some or all of the above symptoms, please be advised that your condition of inner peace may be so far advanced as to not be curable. If you are exposed to anyone exhibiting any of these symptoms, remain exposed only at your own risk.

—Saskia Davis

· 5 ·

MOVING OUT OF PROTECTION

Sometimes when you are protected, you know it. You feel it in your body, and although you may think, "I'd like to learn," somehow the tension, anger, upset, and judgment prevent you from moving into the intention to learn. In this chapter, you will learn some techniques for moving out of protection and into the openness to learn.

12. THE LEARNING LETTER

A very effective way to release protected feelings is to express them in writing. The Learning Letter helps you move through your anger and other blaming "victim" feelings into your fear, your hopes, and then into your love. Once you reach love, you will be in the intention to learn. The purpose of the letter, then, is not so much to help you learn, but to help you move out of the intention to protect and into the intention to learn.

For the most part, when people get angry they get stuck in blaming another person or they turn their anger inwards and get stuck blaming themselves. Expressing your anger when your intention is not to learn will keep you stuck in that anger. But if your intention is to get past your anger and blame and into an open state, then it may be very important for you to express those feelings. The Learning Letter gives you a chance to do that—to really go with your blame, to be in your ego, to be a nasty little kid, to be a victim, or whatever it is. When you get through the feelings, you'll be open. You will find your softness there, and you may find your tears, too.

Even in the middle of an argument you can stop and say, "I don't want to do this. I'm going to write." Then go off by yourself and use the Learning Letter. Stay with it as long as it takes you to write out your feelings. Keep writing until you feel a shift inside of you, moving from the consciousness of being protected to the consciousness of love, the opening of the intention to learn. This shift is definite and you *will* feel it.

You may choose to share the letter with the person to whom you're writing, but its primary use is for you alone. Knowing that no one will see your letter is very freeing, since you don't have to worry about hurting the other person, incriminating yourself, or being judged.

However, if you choose to share your letter with the other person, be clear about your intention. Do you want to get him/her to understand you, feel guilty, or feel afraid? Do you want to change him/her? Do you want him/her to learn? If so, your intention is to protect and you will probably get a defensive response.

Writing is a powerfully cathartic process that takes many people deep into themselves. The letter can be used anytime you're upset. It is a very powerful tool.

To practice this exercise, think of an unresolved conflict in your life that is frustrating or that brings up feelings of being a victim. Find something you have wanted from another person for a long time and haven't gotten. This can be with a mate or ex-mate, parent, child, co-worker, friend, God, yourself—anyone with whom you currently have or once had a problem. If you have trouble coming up with an issue, refer to the list on p. 90.

Next, look over the Learning Letter format. The sentence completions will help you tap into your feelings. In part 1, express all your angry, blaming, and victim feelings. Keep writing until you move into the consciousness of openness. You will know you have reached this place when your body relaxes. Then move on to part 2.

Exercise 12A   How to Write a Learning Letter

A Learning Letter has two parts:

1.   All the blaming feelings that come from your protections.

2.   All the nonblaming feelings that lie under your protections.

Use the following lead-in phrases to help touch off what you are feeling and wanting.

Part 1—Blaming Feelings

These are the feelings that blame someone or something for your condition.

A. Express your anger, irritation, resentment, and criticism:

> I (hate it) (don't like it) when you . . .
>
> I'm (fed up with) (tired of) your . . .
>
> You're just a . . .
>
> You should/shouldn't . . .
>
> It's your fault that . . .
>
> How could you . . .
>
> The problem with you is . . .
>
> I can't stand . . .
>
> If it weren't for you . . .
>
> You make me crazy when you . . .

B. Express your hurt, disappointment, unhappiness, jealousy, and pain—your "poor me" feelings:

> I feel hurt when you . . .
>
> You make me feel . . .
>
> I feel disappointed when you . . .
>
> I feel jealous when you . . .
>
> I feel rejected when you . . .
>
> If it weren't for you . . .
>
> If only you . . .
>
> It's devastating to me when you . . .
>
> I feel so unhappy when you . . .

Continue writing your blaming feelings until you feel yourself shift into the intention to learn. Then go on to part 2.

Part 2—Nonblaming Feelings

These are the feelings that arise when you stop blaming others and take responsibility for the fear and sadness that result from your choices—your part of the difficulty. When expressing nonblaming feelings, the tension will drain from your body and you'll feel soft, open, and vulnerable. Write all you can about your vulnerable feelings, your fears, sadness, and insecurity. Then write about your hopes and your loving feelings. Remember, there is nothing for you to fix. It's okay to feel what you feel without trying to solve a problem.

A. *Fear*. Express your fear, anxiety, and insecurity:

I feel scared when I . . .

I feel scared when you . . .

I feel tense and anxious when you . . .

I feel scared that you don't care about me when you . . .

I'm afraid to let you know how I really feel because . . .

I feel scared that we . . .

B. *Sadness*. Express your sadness over your own choices:

I'm sorry that I . . .

I feel (bad) (awful) when I . . .

I feel sad that I . . .

C. *Hopes*. Express what you want, your dreams and wishes, not your demands:

I often dream that we could . . .

Sometimes I fantasize that . . .

I wish I felt . . .

I wish you felt . . .

I wish that . . .

What I really want is . . .

D. *Love*. Express your love, caring, and understanding:

I love you because . . .

I love it when you . . .

What I love most about you is . . .

Thank you for . . .

I understand that . . .

I appreciate you for . . .

Once you've written your letter, move on to whichever format (chapter 4) you feel would be most helpful to deepen your learning.

13. PASSIVE LISTENING

Passive listening can be used when you are in a conflict and both you and the other person are protected and want to move into the intention to learn, or when you want to move out of your protections but the other person is stuck. The exercise may seem very simple. However, its profoundness may surprise you.

Exercise 13A   How to Listen Passively

All you're going to do is listen while your partner talks for five minutes. In the second part, you'll have a chance to talk for five minutes while your partner listens to you. It may be hard to listen, but it will probably feel wonderful to be listened to. This provides a special opportunity to talk about anything that's on your mind.

If your partner for this exercise is not the person with whom you have the conflict, imagine that your partner is that person and say the things you've been holding back. For example: if you're angry with your mother, tell your exercise partner, "You're going to be my mother and I'm going to talk to you as if you were she." Your partner should simply listen as if he/she is your mother.

For the listener: The listener needs to hear with the heart, not the mind. Eye contact is very important. When the other person is speaking, you will have to resist the tendency to defend and explain yourself. Remember that your partner's silence does not mean agreement or disagreement. You are simply going to listen to each other's feelings.

Before you do this exercise, read the following poem. You may come to understand why being listened to is so rare, and why it feels so good when it happens.

LISTEN

When I ask you to listen to me and you start giving advice,
You have not done what I asked.

When I ask you to listen to me and you begin to tell me why I shouldn't
* feel that way,*
You are trampling on my feelings.

When I ask you to listen to me and you feel you have to do something
to solve my problem,
You have failed me, strange as that may seem.

Listen! All I asked was that you listen, not to talk or do
—just hear me.

Advice is cheap:
twenty-five cents will get you both Dear Abby and Billy Graham
in the same newspaper.

And I can do for myself; I'm not helpless.
Maybe discouraged and faltering, but not helpless.

When you do something for me that I can and need to do for myself,
You contribute to my fear and weakness.

But when you accept as a simple fact that I do feel what I feel,
no matter how irrational, it may seem easier for me to quit trying to
* convince you and I can get about the business of understanding*
* what's behind this seemingly irrational feeling.*

And when that's clear, the answers are obvious and I don't need advice.
* Feelings make sense and are respectable*
when we understand what's behind them.

Perhaps why prayer works, sometimes, for some people,
is because God is mute and doesn't give advice or try to fix things.

Those who care enough to just listen, communicate that they have faith
that you can work things out for yourself.

So, please listen and just hear me. And, if you want to talk, wait a
* minute*
for your turn; and I'll listen to you.

—Anonymous

In the process of talking about your feelings and the situation, you may come up with some new solutions and awarenesses. That is often one of the powerful gifts that comes from being listened to. The answer to all your problems, to all you want to know, is inside you. Nobody else has the answers for you. You just need to find a way to get to your knowing. When you are protected and you don't know how to get out of your protections, you can say, "Okay, let's just have a ten-minute exercise. I'll talk for five minutes, then you talk for five minutes." Then just *listen* to each other; don't be planning what you'll say when it's your turn.

During your time to talk, say anything you want. If you're angry, be angry. If you're blaming, be blaming. If you're a victim, be a victim. You don't have to be open, loving, or in your Higher Self here.

You can talk to one person or to five, if you wish. This is *your* time. Couples don't have to talk about the same issue; each of you can choose anything you want. If you run out of things to say and the other person wants to ask questions, you're probably moving into the intention to learn. This is a listening exercise, not a process for learning. It is a time for releasing feelings so that you can move from protection to openness. Once you feel open, move to whichever format for learning (chapter 4) you feel would be most helpful.

(A variation on this exercise is to set aside twenty minutes; after each person has spoken, each gets another five minutes to speak and listen again. That's how we do it in our workshops.)

14. ACTIVE LISTENING

Active listening differs from passive listening in that the listener offers his interpretations of what the speaker is saying and feeling. This is obviously more difficult than passive listening, since here the listener not only has to be in tune with the speaker but has to give verbal feedback. It's impossible to actively listen when you are protected. When you are not protected but another person is, active listening may help that person to open. When you know that you are protected and you want to move into openness, ask someone to actively listen to you. (We will give you just a brief description of active listening. There are more detailed explanations available in *Parent Effectiveness Training*, by Dr. Thomas Gordon, and *Your Child's Self-Esteem,* by Dorothy Briggs.)

    With active listening, you let the other person know that you understand his feelings by rephrasing or simply restating his feelings and feeding them back with empathy. Being empathic—i.e., feeling with the other—is the most important aspect of active listening. You encourage the other to express all his feelings, both positive and negative. In active listening, you don't ask the other person why he feels a certain way—you just accept his feelings. Your sentences might start off with, "Sounds like you're feeling . . . ," or, "I'm hearing you say that . . ."

It may be easier to understand what active listening is by describing what it is not. It is not:

Asking leading questions
Giving advice
Disagreeing
Explaining
Discounting
Changing the subject
Denying the other's feelings
Denying your own feelings or behavior
Getting angry
Judging
Telling your own stories, feelings
Telling a child how he/she feels
Problem-solving
Lecturing

Condescending
Being distracted or bored
Showing the error in the other's thinking
Placating
Making helpful suggestions
Joking
Exaggerating
Giving examples of the other's behavior
Comparing
Defending
Interrogating
Excusing
Analyzing
Parroting the words
Adding your interpretation
Adding your feelings or ideas

In other words, anytime you respond protectively, you are not actively listening. When you get defensive, try to problem-solve, or attempt to talk others out of their feelings, you miss a wonderful opportunity to learn more about them, and they miss an important opportunity to learn about themselves.

When you listen to another's feelings, some of your feelings may be triggered: fears of inadequacy; problems in your marriage; fears about your parenting and so on. If you find that your feelings prevent you from actively listening to another, explore the situation to learn about what's getting in your way, what fears and beliefs are being tapped into. For example: Are you afraid the speaker's emotions will touch off your own? Do you believe the speaker is not capable of resolving his problems? Are you afraid the speaker can't handle the painful feelings that might come up? Do you believe it will take too much time?

Active listening gives the speaker the feeling of being understood. This is one of the best feelings in the world—like a breath of fresh air, or a sigh of relief that accompanies, "Somebody cares enough to want to understand me."

Feeling understood is vital part of feeling cared about. Not feeling understood almost always keeps protections in place. Once we feel understood, protections often dissolve and we become open to deeper awarenesses.

Exercise 14A   Ways to Practice Active Listening

1.   Ask someone who is close to you to tell you something he is upset about something that has nothing to do with you. Actively listen to him.

2.   Ask the same person or someone else to tell you something he's upset about, something that has to do with you. Actively listen to him.

(You will probably find it easier to actively listen when what the other person is upset about has nothing to do with you. In this way, you can learn a lot about your resistances to active listening.)

3. Ask someone to actively listen to you. You may need to explain to him what active listening is. During the time he is listening to you, you may need to tell him when he's not actively listening.

Remember, this is another tool to move into an *openness* to learn; the learning occurs through your exploration, using a format for learning (chapter 4).

15. POWER STRUGGLES

Power struggles are an inevitable consequence of protections. A power struggle occurs when you try to get something from somebody and he doesn't give it to you. So, you try to get it in another way, or you try the same way again. The harder you try, the more he resists. Power struggles exist in almost all relationships. They can be centered around talking, making love, being on time, cleaning up your room (that's how parents and children get into power struggles very early), doing homework—just about anything.

The real issue at the root of any power struggle is, "I'm not going to be controlled by you." You try to get something from somebody, you try to make something happen; the other person resists because he doesn't want to be controlled by you. You get stuck in an unending circle. You throw up your hands and say, "It seems like such a simple thing. What's the big deal?" The big deal is that someone's integrity is at stake. It has nothing to do with being on time, cleaning your room, or anything like that.

Breaking a power struggle requires letting go, accompanied by the intention to learn. (Permanently breaking a power struggle requires the in-depth learning to be found in exercise 6, "Learning from a Conflict" p. 87.)

This exercise is designed to help you learn about power struggles, your part in perpetuating them, and how to end an argument and become open to learning. The exercise must be done with another person, but not necessarily the person with whom you're in the power struggle. Because there are four parts to the exercise, and it is a little more complicated than most of the others, first read through the entire exercise, then do one part at a time.

In this exercise, you will experience three different interactions: a fight (both people protected), one person changing his intention, and then both people opening to learning—all in five minutes.

Each of you chooses an ongoing issue that you have been upset about, something you have been trying to get from another person for a while. Choose something that's really important to you.

Once you have found your issue, sum up to yourself what you want in one sentence. Examples: "I want you to talk with me." "I need you to make love with me more often." "I want you to be on time." "I want you to do your homework." "I want you to stop taking drugs."

Now decide, for the first round, who will be the Controller and who will be the Resister. (After you go through all four parts of the exercise, you will switch positions so that you each get a chance to be Controller and Resister.)

Exercise 15A Breaking a Power Struggle and Learning from It

Part 1—Protect/Protect

1. *Controller*: You're going to try to get your way, to get the other person to give in to your wishes. You're going to use every verbal device you have ever used and you might even try some new ones. You're going to try to win through creating fear and guilt in the other person.

    Resister: Put your complaint aside for now and come back to it after part 4, when you switch roles. You will not give in to the demands of the Controller and will take a passive but defiant position. You will not be controlled.

2. Stand across from each other, assume your combative postures, and hurl your statements back and forth, e.g.: *Controller*: "I want you to be on time." *Resister*: "Don't you tell me what to do," or simply, "No way!" You will go back and forth, and as the tension mounts, so will your energy.

3. Before you begin, close your eyes for a few moments and get yourselves ready for the ensuing battle. *Controller*: Feel that hard, tight place inside you that

wants to be right and win and that feels the other person is wrong. *Resister*: Feel that tight place inside you that will not be run over. Nobody is going to tell you what to do!

Take two minutes for this part of the exercise.

Part 2—Protect/Open

Resister: Consciously shift your intention to an openness to learning. Respond with statements that come sincerely from this openness ("I don't want to argue, I just want to learn with you," or, "I don't want to argue, I just want to love you"). The first few times, take twenty to thirty seconds to shift your intention and get into the feeling. Close your eyes and take some deep breaths. Feel how much you hate to fight, how much you want to be close and loving, how much it hurts to fight.

Controller: Stay with your desire to win. Continue your statements, holding on to your belief that if you just try harder and find new and creative ways to control, you will eventually get your way.

Take two minutes for this part of the exercise.

Part 3—Open/Open

1. Both partners sit down. *Controller*: Consciously shift your intention to the openness to learning. *Both partners*: Feel how much it hurts to argue, how much you want to be loving and be happy, how tired you are of fighting.

2. Take each other's hands and go back and forth with a loving and learning statement: "I want to be close to you, talk to you, be friends with you, explore with you." Do this for one minute with your eyes closed.

3. Open your eyes and look into each other's eyes while continuing to say your loving and learning words. Feel your own and the other's love and caring.

Do this for one minute (or longer, if you want!).

Part 4—Discussion

Discuss the experience for about five minutes to learn as much as you can from it.

1. *Controller*: Be aware of how it felt in your body when you needed to win and were afraid you would lose. Notice how difficult it was to continue to feel powerfully angry when you got a loving response. How often are you in that situation? How does it feel to soften and open?

2. *Resister*: How did it feel to be in the resistant position? How often and in what situations are you in that position? How did it feel to soften and open?

Parts 5—8:

Reverse roles and do the exercise again.

You can use the idea of shifting your intention anytime you are in an argument and want to break a power struggle so that you can open the door to learning.

If you're in an argument and the other person does not want to learn with you, you can still go away and learn by yourself or with a third person. You can write, call a friend, or do any number of things for yourself. If you believe that you have to have your mate (or whomever you're in conflict with) there in order to learn, you are making yourself into a victim. Remember, *staying in an argument with someone who isn't open is not loving to yourself or to that other person.*

Exercise 15B   Checklist—Self-limiting Beliefs about Being Right or Wrong in a Power Struggle

Often, self-limiting beliefs about right and wrong are at the heart of a power struggle. Who is right and who is wrong? In this situation, the intention to learn will bring you face to face with your fears of being wrong. Take a minute to see which of these beliefs you hold.

____ 1.   If I'm wrong about something, others will think less of me or reject me.

____ 2.   If I'm right, others will love me.

____ 3.   If I make a mistake, it means I'm stupid or not okay, and I'll be rejected.

____ 4.   If I'm right, I'm smart, or okay.

____ 5.   If I'm wrong, I lose.

____ 6.   If I'm right, I win.

____ 7.   It's possible to get love, or get what I want, by being right.

____ 8.   It's better to be right than to be loving.

____ 9.   I must make others see that I am right to make them respect me.

____ 10. I have to make myself wrong to get myself to change.

16. SUMMARY: WAYS TO MOVE OUT OF PROTECTION

1. Write a Learning Letter.
2. Consciously shift your intent: "I don't want to argue, I just want to learn with you" (Exercise 15A).
3. Passively listen.
4. Actively listen.
5. If you are too angry to write or listen:
   A. Express your anger physically, using a pillow or a rolled-up towel and hitting a chair or bed while screaming out your anger. You can also go into a closet or your car and scream.
   B. Do some physical activity, like walking around the block.
   C. Recall an intimate time and the loving feelings you had for another person.
   D. Change your physical environment—i.e., go to a movie or take a bath or shower.
   E. Listen to the tape *You Are Your Higher Self* (see last page of book for details on purchasing) or other guided visualization or progressive relaxation tapes.
   F. Listen to relaxing music.
   G. Allow yourself to feel your sadness and cry.
   H. Play with a pet.
   I. Call a friend and have him/her listen to your anger.
   J. Do a centering prayer/meditation. (Try reading *Open Mind, Open Heart* by Fr. Thomas Keating for this.)
6. Most Important Of All—Take advantage of your new openness to get to the origin of your protective behavior. You cannot go further with your learning without dissolving your protections. The ideas above can be used to patch things up and feelings can be dissolved, but *unless the beliefs that have caused them are cleared up, you will always be at the mercy of your ego*.

ON DEFINING SPIRIT

What then is the spiritual? I find it difficult to define directly. It's much easier to say what it isn't than what it is.

For example—the spiritual is often confused with the moral, but it's not the moral. Morality is concerned with issues of right and wrong. Although often attributed to the "godhead," it actually has a social basis and reflects a social tradition or consensus. What is considered moral varies from culture to culture and from time to time within the same culture. Furthermore, morality often serves as the basis for judgment, for one group of people separating themselves from the other groups, or one individual separating from others. Yet the spiritual is profoundly nonjudgmental and non-separative. The spiritual does not vary from time to time because it is not within time. Spirit is unchanging.

The most important thing in defining spirit is the recognition that spirit is an essential need of human nature. There is something in all of us that seeks the spiritual. This yearning varies in strength from person to person but it is always there in everyone.

—Rachel Naomi Remen

·6·

PROTECTIONS & CONSEQUENCES

Controlling, giving in, rebelling, and becoming indifferent are protective reactions to conflict. In themselves, protections are neither right nor wrong, good nor bad. But protections eventually lead to unhappiness. This chapter will help you understand more about your reactions to conflict and what those reactions create.

Housekeeping, lateness, sexuality, money, in-laws and childraising are just a few of the countless issues that can cause conflict. A more detailed list of conflict issues appears on p. 90.

There are two levels of communication in any conflict: (1) the actual issue of the conflict, and (2) how you react to the conflict.

Picture a garden filled with weeds. You cut the weeds, but the soil is poor and flowers will not grow in it, so the weeds keep coming back. You keep cutting them down and they keep coming back. The weeds are like the *issues* between you, such as communication or money or anything else you argue about. And you keep arguing about them and resolving them and they keep coming up, over and over again. You never directly address *how* you are dealing with the issue.

Once you learn how to learn, you can resolve any issue. It doesn't matter what the issue is. For that reason, we ask you to forget your specific issues for now and concentrate only on your protections. The first step is, of course, to remove the blocks to your being open.

There are two basic categories of conflicts and protections:

1. *Conflict*: Another person does something you don't like and/or think is wrong.

   Protection: You attempt to get that person to change his/her behavior or thinking—i.e., you try to control—or become indifferent.

119

2. *Conflict*: You do something that another person doesn't like and/or thinks is wrong and he/she attempts to get you to change your behavior or thinking.

Protection: You become compliant/rebellious/indifferent or controlling (in trying to get the other person not to be controlling).

Everyone almost always reacts protectively in both of the above situations. Anytime you feel defensive, blaming, self-righteous, shut down, or victimized, you are protected and therefore not open to learning. In fact, *anything other than an intention to learn is protective*. You protect out of fear that you're going to lose something or somebody. As you learn about the ways you protect, it's important not to criticize or judge yourself. We all protect when we're afraid.

What you need to do now is to become aware of the ways in which you protect yourself and to acknowledge that you try to control when you are afraid. Almost all human interactions are about control and manipulation; they are certainly not about learning. This may be hard to face—and even harder when you judge yourself.

17. THE CONTROLLING POSITION: YOUR ATTEMPTS TO CHANGE ANOTHER

We all want others to change, and often it would even be best for them. Wanting change is not the problem; attempting to make others change is what creates the difficulties.

You attempt to control and to manipulate others because you believe that if they would change their behavior, you would be happy and so would they. When people do things you don't like, or you're not getting your way, you think they're wrong or you're afraid for them in some way. Then, believing you are right and they are wrong, you think you have the right to impose your beliefs on them. When your intention is to prove you're right, you're not open to learning.

Most people believe that change comes about by imposing negative consequences—in other words, by creating fear. There's no doubt that people sometimes respond to fear, but there is always a great negative cost to both the person attempting to impose change and the person on the other end of the attempts. Take a good look at your own reactions when people try to get you to change, and the reactions of others around you when you try to get them to change. Notice how effective you are, the results of your efforts. Is it worth it?

Meaningful change without negative consequences occurs through the intention to learn. It's in the process of getting rid of our false beliefs and feeling better about ourselves that the most satisfying changes take place. Change that results from caring, not from fear, leaves everyone feeling more satisfied.

One of the reasons it's so hard to acknowledge controlling behavior is that controlling behavior is painful to other people—it gives them the message that their behavior is wrong. However, inflicting pain on others is not usually your primary intention. You're just trying to protect yourself. We say this not to help you justify your behavior or make it right, but to reduce your self-judgments, which are never helpful.

You may not know right now on a conscious level all the ways you attempt to get others to change. Following is a brief description of some of the typical ways people try to control others. (More detailed descriptions of controlling behavior can be found in *Do I Have to Give Up Me to Be Loved by You?* pp. 165-172, and in *If You Really Loved Me . . .* pp. 57-80.)

Crying. Crying can be a protection when you are crying as a victim. "Poor me. Look what you're doing to me. You're making me feel miserable. You'd better feel guilty." The person who is crying usually is not consciously manipulating. He or she is genuinely upset, but feels like a victim and hopes that the other person will feel guilty and change his behavior.

Not all crying is protective. There are two kinds of tears: those that come from the intention to protect ("Poor me, look what you are doing to me") and those that come from the intention to learn ("Pain is a teacher and I am willing to feel my pain in order to learn").

Telling your feelings. Crying is closely related to telling your feelings. As always, the key is intention. What is your intention in

121

telling your feelings? Is it to learn from your feelings, to learn about yourself, or is it to get another person to change or to justify your feelings? You probably aren't consciously aware of your intention, and likely you've been taught that it is good to express your feelings. However, as with all interactions, the words are less important than the intention. Consider whether you tell others your feelings in order to scare them or make them feel guilty or sorry and thus alter their behavior toward you. Is *your* intention to learn, or is it to get others to learn so that they'll change?

Anger. The message is, "You're bad, you're wrong, and I'm going to be upset with you until you do it my way." The goal here is to frighten the other person into doing things your way.

Pouting. We pout in order to make other people feel guilty, believing that their guilty feelings will cause them to change.

Silence. Silence can be golden, but it can also be filled with tension—the cold shoulder the "look," the evil eye. The message is, "You've done something that's upset me, and this is what you're going to get every time you upset me, until you repent!"

Offering solutions, problem solving. "Why don't you do it this way? If you do, you'll be fine." You're rational and calm, but the intention is still the same—to get the other person to change. When you're trying to solve problems, your intention is not to learn, it's to remain in control, to protect yourself by solving the problem.

Interrogation. "Where were you?" "Who were you with?" You interrogate when you're afraid. You're waiting for the other person to say something you can pounce on. Through interrogation, you gather information you can use in some way or to feel safe.

Being a "nice guy." You act nice to get something or to get someone to be nice to you. (Women can be "nice guys" too.)

Threats. You threaten people at their weakest or most vulnerable points. For example, you threaten physical harm only if they are smaller or weaker than you. Parents who hit their children often say, "I can't help myself. I get upset and it just happens." If the child was six feet tall and weighed 280 pounds, they would probably make a different decision. The same is true with money. You don't threaten to withhold money from a wife who earns as much or more

122

than you do, you use that threat only with someone who is financially dependent on you.

Explaining. "I'll explain to you how wrong you are, show you the error of your ways." When you are lecturing or explaining, especially if no one asked you for an explanation in the first place, your intention may not be to learn anything about yourself or the other person, or to illuminate some issue you are both interested in, but to get the other to "learn" so that he/she will change.

Convincing, or selling yourself. When you say, "But don't you remember the time when . . . ." or "Look at how I've changed," you're defending and promoting yourself rather than opening to learning.

Denial. When you deny, you are actually attempting to determine the other person's reality: "That never happened!" "I don't remember that!"

Criticism. You can disguise hurtful criticism by saying, "This is for your own good," by a sarcastic remark, or by making fun of another. But the message is the same: "You are wrong."

Exercise 17A   How Do You Look and Sound When You're Attempting to Control?

Think about your past and present relationships. Remember times when you were upset because you weren't getting what you needed or wanted and you tried to get others to change their behavior, times when you criticized them, yelled at them, withdrew in anger, or threatened them. Did you want to make them feel guilty or scared? When you are upset, how, specifically, do you try to control people? Do you yell, criticize, or walk away? Are you judgmental, irritated? Do you lecture and explain or tell your feelings? Stop now and think about this.

Get a picture in your mind of how you look when you're upset with another. Whom do you remind yourself of? Is the way you control others similar to the way someone used to control you? Do you treat people the way you were treated as a child? Stop for a while and let the connections happen.

If you're experiencing discomfort now, it's because as you admit to your controlling ways, you're judging yourself as bad or wrong. Remember, you can't learn when you're judging. Remember too that your controlling behavior is your protection.

123

You're not bad or wrong, just scared and unaware. We all control at times. We had to learn behavior as children to survive, and now it's time to learn about them, not judge them. So remind yourself that you have very good reasons for your controlling behaviors—your deep fears of being controlled by others, or of losing their love and being rejected by them.

1. Write down as many different incidents as you can recall in which you attempted to control other people.

2. Again picture yourself in your controlling behavior. Try to see yourself as others see you. Our images of ourselves come mainly from the photographs we've seen of ourselves when we're smiling and open. Most of us never see how we look when we're closed, hard, defensive, and angry. We are very aware of how others look, but we remain blissfully ignorant of ourselves.

3. Try to act out your controlling behavior in front of a mirror. Exaggerate them.

    If you find this too difficult, draw a picture of yourself, or ask others who have witnessed your controlling behavior (spouse, children, employees) to show you how you look.

4. Write about how it feels to realize how controlling you are.

Exercise 17B Checklist—The Ways You Attempt to Control Others

1.   How do I try to control in my relationships?

___ Yell	___ Argue	___ Use sarcasm
___ Criticize	___ Lecture	___ Raise my eyebrows
___ Say "Tsk, tsk"	___ Explain	___ Whine
___ Shake my head	___ Become self-righteous	___ Shrug my shoulders
___ Get annoyed/irritated		___ Make comparisons
___ Accuse	___ Blame	___ Throw things
___ Pout	___ Complain	___ Interrupt
___ Become ill	___ Convince	___ Tell my feelings
___ Be sneaky/deceptive	___ Justify	___ Withdraw angrily
___ Lie/withhold truth	___ Judge	___ Act like a know-it-all
___ Therapize	___ Flatter or give false compliments	___ Interpret
___ Be a "nice guy"	___ Interrogate	___ Teach
___ Give gifts with strings attached	___ Deny	___ Push the other into therapy
___ Sulk	___ Talk others out of their feelings	I use:
___ Take responsibility for others	___ Ask leading questions	___ The silent treatment
___ Moralize	___ Bribery	___ Disapproving looks
___ Nag	___ Scowl	___ Disapproving sighs
___ Analyze	___ Point things out without being asked	___ Blaming tears
___ Be short/curt		___ "Poor me" tears
___ Be indispensable	___ Spank	___ Temper tantrums
___ Give advice	___ Change the subject	___ Put-downs
___ Get angry		___ A superior attitude
		___ Half-truths

Threats of:

___ Financial withdrawal	___ Sexual withdrawal	___ Illness
___ Emotional withdrawal	___ Exposure to others	___ Violence
	___ Abandonment	___ Suicide

Add any other ways you control in your relationships.

2. How do I feel when I am trying to control?

____ Anxious   ____ Unlovable   ____ Deadened, shut
____ Unloving   ____ Lonely   down
____ Empty   ____ One-up   ____ Hurt
____ Righteous   ____ One-down   ____ "Poor me" victim
____ Bad   ____ Frusrated   ____ Martyred
____ Sad   ____ Angry   ____ Sullen
____ Wrong   ____ Weak, tense, uptight
____ Hardened

Exercise 17C   Checklist—Self-limiting Beliefs about Control

____ 1. I can eventually get others to do what I want them to do.

____ 2. The only way I'll get what I want from others is to *make* them do what I want.

____ 3. If I gave up attempting to control others, I'd lose, I'd never get what I need.

____ 4. When I'm right, it's okay to try to make others conform to what I believe.

____ 5. There are no negative consequences of attempting to control.

____ 6. My attempts to control people will eventually earn me their love and appreciation.

____ 7. I can have control over others' liking me, loving me, caring about me, respecting me.

____ 8. I can have control over whether people reject me.

____ 9. My attempts to control my partner won't have any negative effect on his/her desiring to make love with me.

____ 10. I can have control over someone's desiring me sexually.

____ 11. My attempts to control someone can be camouflaged so that they don't know they are being manipulated and there are no negative consequences.

____ 12. I am currently aware of all the ways I attempt to control others, so there is nothing for me to learn in this area.

____ 13. Attempting to control and being in control work to get me what I want. It makes me happy.

____ 14. Since attempting to control others is a sign of caring, they should appreciate it.

____ 15. Controlling behavior is so deeply ingrained that it's impossible to change it.

___ 16. I don't ever attempt to control people in my life.

___ 17. Attempting to have control over others is wrong.

___ 18. I'm bad if I try to control others.

___ 19. Attempting to control through creating guilt and fear in others with my anger, blame, or "poor me" will eventually get me what I want.

___ 20. My anger is something that just happens. I have no control over it.

___ 21. When I'm angry, people should know I'm actually hurt.

___ 22. My anger doesn't hurt others.

___ 23. To attempt to control when I know I'm right is a loving way to be.

___ 24. Attempting to control people works to teach them lessons I want them to learn.

___ 25. Controlling people is a good way to teach them personal responsibility.

___ 26. Being controlling will protect me from being in pain.

___ 27. It feels good to dump my anger on another person.

___ 28. Attempting to control another person is justified when that person does something I feel is wrong.

___ 29. Being angry is a loving thing to do if it's for the other person's own good.

___ 30. I have to stay in control because I don't have a Higher Self to rely on. Everyone else does, but I don't. (Or, there is no such thing as a Higher Self.)

___ 31. I can win in a power struggle.

___ 32. If I don't let people know I'm angry, they won't know how I feel, and they won't pay attention to what I want or consider how I feel.

___ 33. The only way people will take me seriously is if I'm unhappy, depressed, or angry.

___ 34. Judging or criticizing people will get them to change. Once they see I'm right, they'll change.

___ 35. By controlling others, I can make their behavior predictable.

___ 36. If I'm not in control, then I'll be controlled.

18. LOOKING AT COMPLIANCE AND EMOTIONAL CARETAKING

When another person attempts to control you and you attempt to get them to stop, you are trying to control their efforts to control you. In this kind of conflict, there are other protective behaviors that we all manifest. This section will help you become more aware of them.

Note that these protections are not directly controlling; they are your protections in reaction to someone trying to change or control you.

Compliant behavior results from your fear of hurting others' feelings or of them hurting yours. For example, you might make love when you don't feel like it out of fear that your partner will be angry with you or will be hurt by your decision. For the same reasons, you might go along with something your boss wants even though you feel it's unwise or unfair.

Compliant behavior results from fear, obligation, or guilt. Behavior is *not* compliant when it comes from desire and caring. For example, a person may not feel sexual but may still want to make love as an expression of his or her caring feelings.

To "give in" to what the other person wants doesn't fit the definition of loving behavior, because it doesn't nurture your own or the other person's emotional and spiritual growth, and it is not a personally responsible thing to do. People who comply a lot believe it's their job to be emotional caretakers. These are the people who say, "I'm a bad person if I hurt his feelings, so I'll just go along. It's okay."

Many people grow up being caretakers, believing that they have to put their needs aside for other people. They fail to realize that taking responsibility for someone else's feelings doesn't give either person the opportunity to deal with the truth. Caretaking is a trap for both parties involved. It indicates a basic lack of trust in your own and your partner's competency. It means that your actions are based on fear—fear that your partner will fail and it will be your fault, or fear that *you* will fail if you attempt to create your heart's desire. Caretaking out of fear means that you are not being true to yourself, that you are withholding your openness and trust. Without that crucial basis, you will be stuck within a dishonest relationship.

Exercise 18A   How Do You Rationalize Compliance?

When you are giving yourself up, what are you saying in your head? The following statements are examples of how people rationalize compliance:

- Oh, it doesn't really matter. It's not important anyway.

- It's not a big deal.

- It's best for the family.

- I don't want to hurt him, because he can't take it.

- It won't be important tomorrow.

- It's easier than getting into an argument. (Peace at any price. It's easier than telling the truth and seeing what happens.)

- If I don't comply, I could lose him, so I'd better go along.

- I can't have what I really want, so I might as well go along.

- If I say what I want, I'll cause an argument. (In reality, what causes arguments is both people reacting protectively. It is not a matter of who said what to whom.)

- It's what's expected of me.

- It's okay to lose myself, but I can't lose my partner.

- It's the right thing.

Think about how in your life you are being a "good boy" or "good girl. . . ." Do you repress your feelings because you don't want to make people angry? Do you often do what someone wants because you don't want him to disapprove of you or pull away? Do you give up what you want to please others? Stop for a while and feel.

Can you remember a time when you didn't want to do something your partner (or parent, child, boss, or friend) suggested, but went along with it because you were afraid not to? Came home before you wanted to? Spent money on something you didn't want to, or refrained from buying what you wanted? Let someone make love to you when you didn't want to? Take a deep breath now and remember how it feels inside. . . . When you want to say no, and you don't, do you feel weak and frightened? Angry at yourself or at the other person? How does it feel when you let someone else control you?

1. Make a list of all the things that you tell yourself when you comply.

2. Think of situations in which you usually comply. Describe how you look and what you feel about yourself.

3. How do you feel about the other person?

4. What happens between you and the other person when you comply?

129

Exercise 18B   Checklist—The Compliant Position

What are the ways I comply when others attempt to control me, or when I want to avoid their anger?

___ 1.   I don't ask for what I want.

___ 2.   I don't say anything.

___ 3.   I say something is okay with me when it's really not okay.

___ 4.   I don't express my opinion.

___ 5.   I agree with whatever others say.

___ 6.   I give up my own dreams and goals.

___ 7.   I go along with whatever people want me to do.

___ 8.   I give up what I want to do.

___ 9.   I don't stand up for myself.

___ 10.   I give away my power.

___ 11.   I give up knowing what I want so that I don't have to fear not getting it.

___ 12.   I postpone talking about problems.

___ 13.   I do things to please others and get confused about what I want.

___ 14.   I acquiesce.

___ 15.   I take the "easy" way out.

___ 16.   I censor what I say about what I want and how I feel.

___ 17.   I rescue others while ignoring my own needs.

___ 18.   I second-guess or anticipate what others want.

___ 19.   I downplay my needs.

___ 20.   I give in for now, thinking I won't have to next time.

___ 21.   I tell myself that what I want isn't important.

___ 22.   I tell myself that giving in is no big deal.

___ 23.   I tell myself that what I want is wrong.

___ 24.   I tell myself that it's not worth the battle.

___ 25.   I tell myself that I don't deserve it.

___ 26.   I tell myself that it's worth it to get the other person to shut up.

___ 27.   I tell myself that it's better to give in than to hurt someone's feelings.

How do I feel when I protect in this way?

___ Anxious	___ Unlovable	___ Tense, uptight
___ Unloving	___ Lonely	___ Deadened, shut down
___ Empty	___ One-up	
___ Righteous	___ One-down	___ Hurt
___ Bad	___ Frustrated	___ "Poor me"
___ Sad	___ Angry	___ Martyred
___ Wrong	___ Weak	___ Sullen
___ Hardened		

Exercise 18C   Checklist—Self-limiting Beliefs about Compliance

___ 1. Going along with what another person wants will ensure that he/she will love me.

___ 2. I can avoid problems by giving up myself.

___ 3. Giving up myself doesn't lower my self-esteem.

___ 4. Going along with what others want, when it's not what I want, is a loving way to be.

___ 5. There are no negative consequences to behaving out of fear, obligation, or guilt.

___ 6. Love requires doing things that you really don't want to do.

___ 7. Complying is a good way to resolve conflicts.

___ 8. I have to comply or I will lose love. I can't be myself and be loved.

___ 9. A nice person complies in order to make another person happy.

___ 10. Complying will protect me from pain.

___ 11. Complying is more loving than any of the other protections.

___ 12. A good person never walks away from someone who needs him/her.

___ 13. If I do things to make myself happy, I'm selfish. To be unselfish, I have to give up myself to make others happy.

___ 14. If I say no to someone who wants something from me (sex, money, time, affection, attention, etc.), I'm selfish, and I feel guilty and afraid of rejection.

___ 15. Complying with others is a sign of strength. When I go along with what others want I am in my Higher Self.

___ 16. I don't have the right to feel what I feel and want what I want.

___ 17. If I do what I want to make myself happy, bad things will happen to the people I love.

___ 18. If I do what I want to make myself happy, I will end up alone.

19. LOOKING AT RESISTANCE/REBELLION

This behavior occurs when you don't give in and you don't attempt to change another; instead, you resist by rebelling passively or actively.

You're not willing to just say no, but a part of you tightens and says silently, "Don't you tell me what to do!" That part of you may even rebel against your own commands to yourself. For example, when you're on a diet and see something fattening you'd like, one part of you says, "Don't eat that!" and the resistant/rebellious part snatches the forbidden food, saying, "Don't you tell me what to do!" When this rebellious part is passive, you don't do things well or you do them with a lack of enthusiasm, or you "forget" to do them. See if you can tune in to this part of you.
It's when you:

- Say yes and then don't do it.
- Say yes and resent it.
- Say yes with no commitment.
- Procrastinate.
- Make others feel guilty for asking.
- End up saying, "I forgot."
- Do it, but do it badly.

Often, people who tend to be heavily controlling tend also to be very resistant/rebellious, because they're afraid of being dominated.

Think about your relationships. Remember a time when someone wanted you to do something, and you rebelled or withdrew. You refused, saying you weren't in the mood or didn't like the idea . . . . How were you really feeling inside? Is it possible that you wanted to go along but were afraid of looking weak? Did you feel angry at the other person for telling you what to do and stubborn about not giving in? How did the other person react? Did he feel unloved? Rejected? Frustrated? Take a minute to close your eyes and remember the hurt.

Now remember another time when someone wanted something from you . . . and inside you felt a voice saying, "Don't give in, don't do what he wants, or he'll control you forever." How do you feel about yourself when you're resistant/rebellious? Stop and feel.

Exercise 19A   Checklist—The Resistant/Rebellious Position

1.   What are the ways I resist when someone attempts to control me?

___ 1.   I say I'll do what he/she wants and then I don't do it.

___ 2.   I do the opposite of what he/she wants.

___ 3.   I explain, defend, or get mad about why I shouldn't do it.

___ 4.   I get critical and make the other person wrong for asking.

___ 5.   I say I'll do it and then I do something else.

___ 6.   I say I'll do it and then I forget, or I fail to show up.

___ 7.   I procrastinate.

___ 8.   I act helpless or incompetent.

___ 9.   I get apathetic—no enthusiasm.

___ 10. I get sick.

___ 11. I give to pets or friends what the other person has asked of me.

___ 12. I misunderstand, or am unable to understand.

___ 13. I do it, but only halfway.

___ 14. I do it wrong on purpose.

___ 15. I find some way to sabotage the situation.

___ 16. I pretend not to hear.

___ 17. I'm disinterested.

___ 18. I'm not open to learning.

___ 19. I won't make a commitment.

2.   How do I feel when I protect in this way?

___ Anxious	___ Unlovable	___ Tense, uptight
___ Unloving	___ Lonely	___ Deadened, shut
___ Empty	___ One-up	down
___ Righteous	___ One-down	___ Hurt
___ Bad	___ Frustrated	___ "Poor me"
___ Sad	___ Angry	___ Martyred
___ Wrong	___ Weak	___ Sullen
___ Hardened		

3.   What happens between me and another person when I resist/rebel?

Exercise 19B   Checklist—Self-limiting Beliefs about Rebellion

___ 1.   Rebelling is a good way to establish my independent identity.

___ 2.   My only choices when another person is attempting to control me are to comply or to rebel.

___ 3.   There are no negative consequences to resisting or rebelling.

___ 4.   I really am being my own person when I rebel.

___ 5.   It's the controlling person's fault that I resist or rebel.

___ 6.   Resisting and rebelling are automatic responses that just happen. I can't do anything about it.

___ 7.   Rebelling and resisting will eventually work to get the other person off my back.

___ 8.   My self-esteem is not lowered when I resist and rebel.

___ 9.   To resist and rebel when I know I'm right is a loving way to be.

___ 10.   Rebelling will protect me from pain.

___ 11.   My rebelling doesn't hurt anyone.

___ 12.   By resisting and rebelling, I can avoid being controlled.

___ 13.   When I don't want to do what others want me to do, they will not stop pressuring me unless I rebel.

___ 14.   Rebelling is the only way to establish what I want. Otherwise, no one will hear me.

___ 15.   Rebelling is the only way to get people's attention.

___ 16.   If I didn't resist and rebel, I would be controlled or swallowed up.

20.   LOOKING AT RESISTANCE/INDIFFERENCE

When you are afraid of domination, you may resist by becoming indifferent. You don't want to give the other person the upper hand, nor do you want to give up yourself.

Indifference doesn't involve trying to change others, doesn't even engage others, but merely allows you to disappear emotionally and physically. Almost anything can be used to shut down and avoid facing difficult situations or feelings—drugs or alcohol, work, sleep, reading, illness, TV, food, sports, meditation. None of the things you use to shut down is inherently protective; it depends on your intention. Watching TV to relax is not protective unless your intent in watching TV is to block out your feelings or to avoid interacting with others.

Look at the ways you spend your time and see how much of it is devoted to avoiding something else. For example, when you find yourself standing in front of the refrigerator looking for something to eat when you're not hungry, what would you have to confront if you didn't eat anything?

Exercise 20A   Checklist—The Resistant/Indifferent Position

1.   What do you use to shut down or to ignore other people?

___ Work	___ Sex	___ Reading
___ Drugs/alcohol	___ TV	___ Sports
___ Hobbies	___ Children	___ Friends
___ Illness	___ Food	___ Sleep
___ Meditation	___ Storytelling	___ Fantasizing
___ Spending money	___ Worrying	___ Daydreaming

Fill in other ways you shut down or ignore others:

(When you need these behaviors to feel good or to relieve pain, you become obsessed with them, like an addiction.)

2.   How do you feel about yourself when you become indifferent and/or avoid others? (Make a list.)

3.   How do other people react to such behavior?

4.   How do their reactions leave you feeling?

Exercise 20B   Checklist—Self-limiting Beliefs about Indifference

___ 1.   I can shut down and still enjoy life.

___ 2.   I can shut down and still have intimacy.

___ 3.   Indifference will protect me from feeling pain.

___ 4.   My indifference doesn't hurt anyone. It it not unloving.

___ 5.   I can avoid problems by becoming indifferent.

___ 6.   I can avoid being controlled by becoming indifferent.

___ 7.   Becoming indifferent is more loving than any of the other protections.

___ 8.   Being indifferent does not lower my self-esteem.

___ 9.   If I become indifferent, the problem will take care of itself.

___ 10.   It's better to be shut down and to withdraw than to reach out and risk rejection.

21.   CONSEQUENCES OF PROTECTIONS

When you decide to be protected, there are certain things that inexorably follow. It probably doesn't feel as though you decide, because protections happen instantaneously. However, you are always making decisions about how you will behave, whether you are going to go with your ego or with your Higher Self. You *always* have that choice. It is your will that decides. If you insist that you don't have a choice, that everything just "happens" to you, then you don't have to take responsibility for the conditions that you create.

Most people think, "I am in pain because . . . "

- He won't talk to me.
- He doesn't open up with me.
- She doesn't want to connect with me.
- She gets angry with me.
- He doesn't work as hard as I want him to.
- I don't have a partner and I'm alone.
- The only way I can be happy is if I'm connected with somebody else.

Can you see the "victimness" of all the above thoughts?

Seeing the connection between your unloving behavior and the negative consequences it produces is one of the most powerful motivations to bring about change. This means acknowledging the consequences of your decision to be protected—the consequences to you personally and to your relationships. The realization that all of the pain in our lives results from unloving behavior gives us a very powerful, parallel awareness: only love can create meaningful change in our lives.

Here are some of the seriously painful consequences of staying in your protections:

- You feel deadened when you shut down and become indifferent.
- You feel bad about yourself when you give in, injure others, or resist and rebel.
- You feel alienation from others as well as from yourself.
- You lose touch with your true nature and either settle into a lifeless existence or devote all your time to achieving material success which never gives you true joy.
- Your relationships become unsatisfying, and you either settle for much less than you want; or you make fleeting connections that give you temporary happiness but leave you disappointed and unfulfilled.

You may feel your pain intensely, or you may be just barely aware of a dull ache inside. Either way, few people connect their pain directly to their own choices to protect themselves.

The most important thing to look at in terms of negative consequences is how you end up feeling about yourself. Is your self-esteem being raised by your protections, or is it being lowered?

Following are a few of the responses that came from workshop participants when we asked them to share the consequences of their protections. Comments from Jordan and Margie are in parentheses.

"My body is bent out of shape. It hurts. I feel tense, tight, sick."

"I feel needy and helpless."

"I don't like the person I become. I feel bad right now just thinking about it."

"I feel hateful. Everyone goes away. I end up feeling alone, alienated from other people and myself."

"I lose my peace, my centeredness."

"I feel deadness." (You feel deadened because you're not connecting with yourself. You are protected from yourself.)

"I have to do a lot of managing. Life is hard."

"I'm uncreative, tight, and tense, and everything is hard. Confused and immobilized. I lose touch with my own knowing. I can't find my Higher Self when I'm in this tense, protected situation, so how can I know what I want?"

"I feel scared, worthless, depressed." (Depression, a consequence of protections, is present in our country on a vast scale. Look at the amount of drugs people take for depression. We say, "I'm depressed because of something out there," rather than, "I'm protecting myself and depression is the consequence.")

"I feel confused. I look inside and nothing is there. It's empty. I don't know what I want or what I feel." (You cannot know what you want and feel when you're coming from the ego. You can know only from the Higher Self, and you have to be willing to feel your pain in order to do that.)

Your automatic reaction in a conflict is frequently the worst reaction because it will almost always be unloving. Skiing provides a good analogy for understanding our automatic protections. When you come to a steep run, the typical reaction is to tense up and hold your breath. You may or may not get down the slope without falling, but if you stay in your fear and tension, the process of getting down is going to be hard work. To get down the slope with ease and grace, with the connected flowing motion of the expert skier, you need to breathe out and to open. *Open!* Instead of your normal reaction, which is to tense up, you need to do exactly the opposite to stay centered, to flow.

The same thing is true in conflict. When you believe you can't handle difficult situations, you protect to avoid your present pain and your feared future pain. The paradox is that your protections bring about the pain. You're stuck on a treadmill, having to deal with the same problems over and over again.

When you're having a particularly difficult time with someone in your life, instead of trying to change him or figure him out, shift the focus to yourself. Ask yourself, "What is that person in my life to teach me? What do I need to learn?"

Exercise 21A   The Consequences of Your Protections

Think about a current relationship in your life—with a mate, a child, a parent, a friend, a boss, or an employee. Remember a time when you tried to control that person with your anger, silence, criticism, blame, lectures, threats, tears, or any other of the ways you control. Notice the details of the situation: Where were you? Who else was around? What triggered it? How did the other person react? Did he/she cry, get angry or get very quiet? Did he/she do what you wanted or did he/she resist and rebel against you?

How were you feeling inside when you behaved in these ways? What happens in your body—your stomach, your throat, your head? How do you feel about yourself when you are upset with someone and you try to control him? Do you ever feel embarrassed afterward? Do you ever feel hopeless or helpless? How does it make you feel to know that people you care about are afraid to upset you? Does it make you feel powerful, or does it depress you? Does it make you feel lovable or unlovable? Close your eyes and answer these questions honestly.

Now take a deep breath and let all those thoughts go. Remember a time in a present relationship when someone wanted you to do something and you complied or withdrew or rebelled. Choose only one incident and remember it in as much detail as possible.

Take another breath and remember how you felt inside. Did you feel weak, frightened, tense, anxious, angry at yourself or at the other person? When you go along with what the other person wants or when you resist or withdraw, rather than decide what you want for yourself, do you feel weak and unlovable? Feel that sensation in your body. Stop and give yourself time to feel.

And now think about what happens between you and the other person. What is the outcome of complying or rebelling or withdrawing? Do you feel loving toward the other person? Do you feel loved? Even if you avoid conflict by complying, do you end up feeling loved and loving? When you rebel or withdraw, how does the other person react? Does he get angry?

Feel within you the many consequences of your protections and write about how you're feeling and what you're learning.

Exercise 21B   The Consequences of Your Protections in a Current Conflict

For this exercise, either write the scenario, say it into a tape recorder, or play-act both parts. Play-acting offers some great benefits: if you can really get into doing your partner's physical postures and behaviors, you will get a deeper understanding of how your partner feels and possibly of what he/she thinks, too. You may also begin to see some humor in the situation, strange as it may sound!

1. Pick an ongoing conflict in your life and make up a script detailing the interaction. Start with the conflict. (For example, you want to make love and your partner isn't in the mood. If you can't think of a conflict, review the list on p. 90.) Describe or act out your behavior, your partner's reaction, and your reaction to your partner's reaction. Be sure to include physical reactions, too. (Do you avoid looking at each other? Do you frown, get a tight look, or go red in the face?)

2. See if you can write or act what you're feeling with each response and what your partner is feeling. You can probably re-create the words exactly as they have occurred and will occur in the future.

3. Continue this process, using other conflict issues in your life. Do as many as you can, as intensely as you can, until you *know* that your protections will always produce the same negative results. (As long as you have hope that your protections will work, you will continue them.)

Exercise 21C   Checklist—Negative Consequences of Protections

Select the lists (A through D) that apply to your relationships and check the statements that apply. Feel free to add your own. List E, "Negative Consequences to Yourself," applies to everyone.

A. Negative Consequences with a Partner (or Past Partner)

___ 1. Our sex is infrequent and/or boring, with no passion or love.
___ 2. Our relationship is boring, routine, with little excitement or intensity.
___ 3. There is a feeling of distance between us.
___ 4. My partner feels insecure about my love.
___ 5. I feel unloved and/or insecure about my partner's love.
___ 6. I feel unloving.
___ 7. There is a lack of satisfying communication.
___ 8. I like myself better when I am not around my partner.
___ 9. My partner and I don't have much fun together.
___ 10. I feel freer when my partner is not around.
___ 11. Nothing seems important or exciting to my partner.
___ 12. I feel resistant, rebellious, resentful a lot of the time.
___ 13. My partner is often resistant, rebellious, resentful.
___ 14. I often lie or don't tell things to my partner.
___ 15. My partner often lies or doesn't tell me things.
___ 16. I often feel guilty around my partner.
___ 17. My partner seems to act out of obligation.
___ 18. I feel manipulated.
___ 19. We're in a power struggle, each wanting only to win.
___ 20. I feel on guard around my partner.
___ 21. I don't feel valued for my accomplishments.
___ 22. I don't share my partner's enthusiasms.
___ 23. My partner doesn't share my enthusiasms.
___ 24. Our conflicts do not reach satisfying resolutions.
___ 25. I feel jealous or envious.

B. Negative Consequences with a Child

___ 1. We have constant power struggles.
___ 2. I feel a lack of caring toward my child.

___ 3.   My child doesn't care about me.

___ 4.   My child is often angry or irritable with me.

___ 5.   I often feel angry or irritable with my child.

___ 6.   My child is often resistant, defiant, rebellious.

___ 7.   We have frequent hassles over chores, homework, etc.

___ 8.   My child has low self-esteem.

___ 9.   My child is doing poorly in school.

___ 10. My child is often fearful, lacks confidence.

___ 11. My child is often rejected by peers.

___ 12. My child is self-abusive.

___ 13. My child is abusive with other people and/or things.

___ 14. There is an emotional distance between me and my child.

___ 15. I feel inadequate as a parent.

C. Negative Consequences with Your Parent

___ 1.   We get into power struggles.

___ 2.   I feel controlled by my parent.

___ 3.   I feel the weight of obligations to my parent.

___ 4.   I feel emotionally shut down or dead around my parent.

___ 5.   I can't talk to my parent.

___ 6.   I feel rejected by my parent.

___ 7.   I feel inadequate in my parent's eyes.

___ 8.   I feel angry or irritated with my parent.

___ 9.   I feel unloving toward my parent.

___ 10. I feel misunderstood by my parent.

___ 11. I feel unloved by my parent.

D. Negative Consequences in the Workplace

___ 1.   I'm involved in one or several power struggles at work.

___ 2.   I lack interest and motivation.

___ 3.   I feel manipulated.

___ 4.   I feel resistant, rebellious.

___ 5.   I feel angry, annoyed, and/or resentful.

___ 6.   I feel critical, judgmental.

___ 7.   I feel used, taken advantage of.

___ 8.   I feel unappreciated and/or unimportant.

___ 9. I feel isolated.

___ 10. I feel inadequate and/or scared.

___ 11. I feel trapped.

___ 12. I'm chronically late.

___ 13. My employee or partner is often late.

___ 14. My employee or partner is resistant.

___ 15. My employee or partner has lost initiative and motivation.

E. Negative Consequences to Yourself

___ 1. I am frequently ill.

___ 2. I repeat similar patterns in my relationships.

___ 3. I have difficulty in connecting with others.

___ 4. I'm attracted to people who are unavailable.

___ 5. I'm alone. I feel isolated.

___ 6. I have low self-esteem, feel inadequate and unlovable.

___ 7. I feel tension, fear, anxiety, frustration, anger, guilt.

___ 8. I feel depressed, deadened, apathetic, sad, bored.

___ 9. I feel unloving.

___ 10. I feel manipulated.

___ 11. I feel smothered.

___ 12. I feel rejected.

___ 13. I often experience a lack of commitment in relationships.

___ 14. I have little creativity.

___ 15. I lack joy.

___ 16. I feel powerless.

Exercise 21D   Checklist—Self-limiting Beliefs about Protections and Consequences

Go over this checklist very carefully. Remember that all of these statements are erroneous. Each one that you check is worthy of many hours of exploration.

Part 1   Protections

___ 1. My protections will eventually get me what I want.

___ 2. My protections work to avoid pain.

___ 3. My protections are not unloving.

_____ 4. It's possible to be protected and still be intimate and connected.

_____ 5. It's possible to be protected and open to learning at the same time.

_____ 6. It's possible to be protected and feel happy.

_____ 7. It's possible to be protected without eroding my self-esteem.

_____ 8. It's possible to be protected and feel adequate.

_____ 9. It's possible to be protected and feel lovable.

_____ 10. Being unprotected leaves me too vulnerable.

_____ 11. If I'm open and loving, people will take advantage of me.

_____ 12. Being soft and open is being weak. People will think less of me.

_____ 13. Being protected feels good.

_____ 14. Being protected is really taking care of myself.

_____ 15. Being protected has no negative consequences.

_____ 16. I have to protect because people don't care about me.

_____ 17. Being protected is the way I can feel powerful.

_____ 18. When I protect, I'm owning my personal power.

_____ 19. It's important to be protected in order to teach the other person a lesson. If I'm not protected, others will think they can get away with their unloving behavior.

Part 2 Consequences

_____ 1. My feelings are not a result of my own choices. My feelings are a result of how other people treat me.

_____ 2. My unhappiness is caused by how others treat me.

_____ 3. It's my partner's, or my parents', or someone else's fault that:

    _____ I have a lousy sex life.

    _____ I have no fun.

    _____ I have no intimacy in my life.

    _____ I'm alone.

    _____ I have no money.

    _____ We never talk.

    _____ My kids are screwed up.

    _____ I never have time for myself.

    _____ I'm unhappy.

    _____ I feel bad about myself.

___ I'm overweight.

___ I'm always late.

___ I'm a failure.

___ I'm sick a lot.

4. It's my fault, or I'm no good, because:

___ I don't like my life.

___ I can't change.

___ I'm not happy.

___ I'm so judgmental and critical.

___ People don't like me.

___ I'm not successful.

5. Fill in your own:

_____

_____

_____

_____

DO YOU ACT — OR REACT?

I walked with my friend, a Quaker, to the newsstand the other night, and he bought a paper, thanking the newsie politely. The newsie didn't even acknowledge it.

"A sullen fellow, isn't he?" I commented.

"Oh, he's that way every night," shrugged my friend.

"Then why do you continue to be so polite to him?" I asked.

"Why not?" inquired my friend. "Why should I let him decide how I'm going to act?"

As I thought about this incident later, it occurred to me that the important word was "act." My friend acts towards people; most of us react towards them.

He has a sense of inner balance which is lacking in most of us; he knows who he is, what he stands for, how he should behave. He refuses to return incivility for incivility, because then he would no longer be in command of his own conduct.

When we are enjoined in the Bible to return good for evil, we look upon this as a moral injunction—which it is. But it is also a psychological prescription for our emotional health.

Nobody is unhappier than the perpetual reactor. His center of emotional gravity is not rooted within himself, where it belongs, but in the world outside him. His spiritual temperature is always being raised or lowered by the social climate around him, and he is a mere creature at the mercy of these elements.

Praise gives him a feeling of euphoria, which is false, because it does not last and it does not come from self-approval. Criticism depresses him more than it should, because it confirms his own secretly shaky opinion of himself. Snubs hurt him and the merest suspicion of unpopularity in any quarter rouses him to bitterness.

A serenity of spirit cannot be achieved until we become the masters of our own actions and attitudes. To let another determine whether we shall be rude or gracious, elated or depressed, is to relinquish control over our own personalities, which is ultimately all we possess. The only true possession is self-possession.

—Sidney J. Harris

· 7 ·

ACKNOWLEDGING & RESPECTING FEAR

We've all been taught that it's wrong or weak to be afraid, so most of us cover our fears with protections. When we compare ourselves to others, we believe we're the only ones who are afraid or that others are less afraid than we are. Let's start by acknowledging that everyone has many deep fears. We have all come to believe that we're not good enough, not lovable, inadequate, not "doing it" right, or just plain hopeless. From these beliefs come the fears of disapproval, rejection, abandonment, and domination, from which we protect ourselves in relationships.

You may not want to believe it, but everyone suffers from the same fears—your spouse, your boss, the minister who guides you, the psychologist whose counsel you seek, the president in whom you put your trust. Some people hide their fears better than others and even attain success in spite of them, but when you know people intimately, you discover that we're all in this thing together. The demons of self-doubt affect us all, especially in relationships.

You are not wrong for being afraid. As children, disapproval or rejection was a life-or-death issue and as adults, it still feels the same way. You may often feel panic in the face of disapproval and go far out of your way to avoid it.

But you *can* move past your fears. You have already moved past many of them. Think of the things you were afraid of in the past that no longer control your life—driving a car, riding a bike, or starting a new job. You can move past many more fears, too, but you will be seriously hampered if you judge yourself for being afraid. Be kind to yourself. Know that your fears are always generated by your erroneous, self-limiting beliefs. These beliefs are the very important reasons for your feelings, thoughts, and behavior, and that looking at them without judgment will greatly accelerate your emotional growth.

If you weren't afraid, you would be as open as a newborn. When confronted with something, you wouldn't be concerned with being "wrong," you would merely react with curiosity: "Oh, that's interesting. Why am I feeling this way? And what do I have to learn in this situation? What's my lesson here?"

You could approach any situation in your life with that kind of curiosity if you weren't afraid of being wrong or inadequate. But you close to learning, especially to learning about yourself, when you fear looking inside and finding things about yourself that you think are bad.

Most of us spend a great deal of energy hiding the part of ourselves that we believe is ugly or bad, fearing that this "bad" part is proof that we're no good, that we're unlovable, that we're to blame and it's all our fault. Since we don't want it to be our fault, we close down and point at the other person, saying, "It's all *your* fault." We focus on trying to get others to look inward so that we won't have to. To be open to learning, you must be ready to say, "Okay, I'm willing to take full responsibility." You must be willing to stop trying to get the other person to "see" anything and focus on what you are doing to create your own happiness or unhappiness. Then you can truly be open to learning.

Having stopped yourself from saying, "Well, she's got a part in this," or, "If it weren't for him. . ." you will open to taking total responsibility. You will say instead, "What's my lesson here? What do I need to learn? What's my part in this?" This is very difficult as long as you believe that being responsible means being wrong. From this belief follows the fear that if you're wrong, the other person won't love you and you'll lose something of value—yourself or the other person.

We all have within us a child who still believes that if we aren't loved, we can't survive. When someone is angry or upset with us, we become like a five-year-old saying, "Uh-oh. I'm wrong, I'm bad, it's my fault, they're going to be angry, they're going to abandon me, and I'm going to die." We desperately cling to the false belief that if someone rejects us, we can't handle it. This in turn creates the false belief that our unhappiness is tied to the other person, rather than to our own behavior.

22. FEARS ABOUT RELATIONSHIPS WITH OTHER PEOPLE

Our deepest fears and false beliefs are triggered in the relationships that are most important to us. All our protections come from the fear of these people, who have a power similar to that of our parents. (You probably give power to everyone who plays an important part in your life.) Therefore, when any of these important people disapprove of you, those fears are touched off. Most people find it much easier to be open to learning anywhere other than in their important relationships, particularly their primary relationships.

Exercise 22A   Exploring Fears about Relationships with Other People

1.   Think about the fears you have regarding relationships in general or in some of the particular relationships in your life.

2.   Complete any or all of the following sentences:
     Some of the fears I have about being in a relationship are . . .
     Some of the fears I have about my relationship with (name of person) are . . .
     Some of the fears I have about being in a relationship with my boss, peers,
        siblings, parents, or children are . . .

If you are alone, speak your thoughts or write them down. Do as many as you can in five minutes.

If you have a partner, you can do this out loud together. Your partner will say one of his/her fears, then you'll say one of yours; and go back and forth like that for ten minutes. Don't analyze, discuss, or caretake.

EXAMPLES: A fear I have about being in a relationship with my husband is that everything is going to be up to me; that if we're going to be connected or if we're going to learn, it's always going to be up to me, it will be all my responsibility.

151

A fear I have about being in a relationship with my wife is that she is too powerful and she'll be in control of the situation because she talks about her feelings easier than I do, and if we get into talking about feelings, I will be overwhelmed.

When I was a kid, a fear that I had about being in relationships with my friends was that I was going to be left out, that I wasn't important enough to be included.

Exercise 22B   Checklist—Self-limiting Beliefs about Being Vulnerable

____ 1.   If I show people my true feelings, they won't care about me.

____ 2.   No one cares about my true feelings.

____ 3.   If I show people my sadness, I'll be rejected and end up in even more pain.

____ 4.   People who are soft and open get trampled and beaten down.

____ 5.   If I'm soft and open, people will see me as weak and lose respect for me.

____ 6.   If I'm honest about my true feelings, people will use my feelings against me.

____ 7.   If people see my true feelings, they will think I'm childish and immature.

____ 8.   People will judge me if I'm vulnerable and tell them how I really feel.

____ 9.   If I'm open and trusting, I'll get sucked in and duped. Then people will think I'm stupid and reject me.

____ 10. If I'm open and vulnerable I'll get run over and give myself up.

23.   FEARS ABOUT INADEQUACY

Some of the most devastating erroneous beliefs you learned in childhood had to do with your adequacy. When your natural expressions were met with disapproval—when you heard, "You mean, that hurt your feelings?" or, "I'll give you something to cry about," you came to believe you were too sensitive. When you heard, "Calm down, don't get so excited," or, "You ask too many questions," you came to believe there was something wrong with you for feeling as you did or for your curiosity. When you expressed your natural sexual curiosity, you got negative messages about that, too. Many things about your behavior seemed wrong because they didn't fit what the adults around you believed was right. How often did you get the message that you were wrong in regard to your eating or grooming habits, or how you chose to spend your time? To be lovable often meant to be exactly what the adults around you expected you to be. To be lovable meant to be perfect (by their standards/beliefs), and you didn't measure up.

The messages you received were often nonverbal. You may simply have gotten a feeling that something was wrong, rather than having heard the words. The messages may have come not only from your parents but also from siblings, grandparents, other relatives, teachers, and friends, as well as from books, television, and radio. We all came to conclusions about our inadequacy. There was a right way to think, feel, act, and look, and we weren't cutting it. So we learned early in our lives to adjust to being imperfect, unlovable, inadequate, and wrong.

Go deep inside and ask yourself: What messages did I receive in my childhood? Maybe no one ever said you were wrong. Maybe you just concluded as much from what your parents did or didn't do. Maybe the message was, "I'll love you if you are good," or "You're not good enough because you're a girl," or, "You've always been nothing but trouble." Recall how you felt about those messages. Did they hurt, make you angry, or make you want to hide? How are those messages still affecting you today? Are you acting out those same childhood roles? Are you still a good little girl? Are you still a troublemaker? Are you still an underachiever? Stop and let yourself feel now. . . .

Exercise 23A   Exploring Fears about Inadequacy

1. Do I fear being seen as:

A failure	Successful	Sick
Wrong	Inadequate	Unacceptable
Incompetent	Unmasculine	Immature
Stupid, dumb	Unfeminine	Neurotic
Ugly	Selfish	Foolish
Shy, timid	Boring	Closed

2. Do I believe that another person will not meet my needs because I'm:

Unworthy	Inadequate	Unlovable
Incompetent	Too poor	Not good enough

3. What messages did I get in childhood about being good or bad, right or wrong, okay or not okay?

4. What do I believe isn't good enough about me now? Do I feel inadequate physically, intellectually, emotionally, or socially? Do I believe there's something wrong with my personality, that I'm not creative enough, or that I don't have a sense of humor?

5. Do I feel unsure of myself because:

    A. I believe I am not as intelligent, articulate, wealthy, attractive, interesting, independent, creative, social, open, or important as my partner, as other people, or as I should be?

    B. I am too old, too young, too sensitive, too intense, or too timid?

6. Are these beliefs causing me pain? If so, how do I protect from the pain of these beliefs?

7. Why do I continue to believe this way? What am I afraid would happen if I let go of these beliefs?

Exercise 23B   Checklist—Self-limiting Beliefs about Adequacy and Lovability

___ 1.   I'm not adequate.

___ 2.   I'm not lovable.

___ 3.   I'm not good enough.

___ 4.   I'm basically a bad, unworthy person.

___ 5.   My adequacy, lovability, and feelings of self-worth and self-esteem come from other people liking or approving of me.

___ 6.   I'm inadequate, unlovable, or not good enough because:

> ___ I'm too tall.
>
> ___ I'm too short.
>
> ___ I'm too thin.
>
> ___ I'm too fat.
>
> ___ I'm ugly, homely, or unattractive.
>
> ___ I'm not intelligent enough.
>
> ___ I'm not creative enough.
>
> ___ I don't have a good sense of humor.
>
> ___ I don't make enough money.
>
> ___ I don't drive a nice car.
>
> ___ I'm shy.
>
> ___ I'm too aggressive.
>
> ___ I'm too selfish.
>
> ___ I'm too intense.
>
> ___ I'm too much, but I'm not sure what I'm too much of.
>
> ___ I'm too intelligent.
>
> ___ I'm too different.
>
> ___ I'm weird.
>
> ___ I'm scattered.
>
> ___ I make mistakes.
>
> ___ I have physical defects or imperfections.
>
> ___ I have problems.
>
> ___ I cry too easily.
>
> ___ I'm too emotional.
>
> ___ I'm not perfect.
>
> ___ I'm not very talkative.

___ I don't think quickly enough.

___ I don't agree with you.

___ I'm just like my father.

___ I'm just like my mother.

___ I can't take care of myself.

___ I need a man to take care of me.

___ I need a woman to take care of me.

___ I can't make decisions.

___ I'll never amount to anything.

___ I can't tell jokes well.

___ I'm too serious.

___ I'm not serious enough.

___ I'm too sensitive.

___ I'm too insensitive.

___ I always make a bad first impression.

___ I think differently from other people.

___ I'm a loner.

___ I don't have a partner.

___ I'm afraid to be alone.

___ I have fears.

___ I have phobias.

___ I'm immature.

___ I'm not a professional.

___ I never went to college.

___ I didn't graduate from high school.

___ I have a small vocabulary.

___ I can't do math.

___ I don't read well.

___ I have too much imagination.

___ I have no imagination.

___ I'm too spiritual.

___ I'm not spiritual enough.

___ I can't do anything right.

___ When bad things happen, it's always my fault.

___ Bad things always happen to me.

___ I'm a compulsive overeater.

___ I'm an alcoholic.

___ I'm a drug addict.

___ I'm too sexual.

___ I'm a sex addict.

___ I'm not sexual enough.

___ I'm crazy.

___ I'm a phony.

___ I'm righteous and arrogant.

___ I'm depressed.

___ I'm lazy.

___ I'm superficial.

___ I'm screwed up.

___ I'm not important.

___ I'm boring.

___ I'm second-rate.

___ I have no personality.

___ I'm a goody-goody.

___ I'm stupid.

___ I don't want to be in a committed relationship.

Exercise 23C   Fears about Learning

1.   Take a minute to look inside. Think about what you are afraid is wrong with you: your imperfections; your fear of being wrong; what you feel inadequate about; your fears about being inadequate, not enough, not important, not lovable. Think about what you protect yourself from knowing about yourself.

2.   Complete the following sentence: "A fear I have about being open to learning about myself is. . . ."

EXAMPLE: I have a fear that if I open to learning about myself, I'll find out I'm wrong, and wrong means bad, unlovable. It is going to confirm that there really is something bad or unlovable about me, and that's why I have difficulty in being open to learning. (Keep expanding into the depths of your feelings and beliefs.)

24. FEAR OF PAIN

A great deal of our behavior boils down to trying to avoid pain. There will be some pain in being open. As long as you believe you can't handle it, you will remain closed to learning.

In their well-meaning but often misguided attempts to be loving, parents often give many verbal and nonverbal messages that it is bad or wrong to be in pain and/or that their children can't handle deep pain. Attempts to smooth over painful events by getting children to stop feeling their pain, glossing over it or trying to make it better, all communicate that it is not right to feel pain and that you can't handle your own pain. Parents who fall apart when their children are hurt or scared communicate that they can't handle their children's pain; therefore, the child must avoid or not show pain.

It is very rare for parents to caringly communicate that they have confidence that their children can find their way through pain and learn from it.

What are your fears of being in pain? If you let yourself open to deep pain—for example, the pain of rejection—what do you believe would happen to you? That you'll go crazy? That you can't handle it? That it will overwhelm you?

In truth, you can handle a great deal of pain, and you don't have to be afraid of it. The thought of being in pain is worse than the reality, but until you test out your beliefs about pain you will stay stuck in protecting yourself.

Exercise 24A   Exploring Fear of Pain

Do you fear feeling:

Afraid	Hurt	Disappointed
Humiliated	Weak	Grieved
Criticized	Disoriented	Insecure
Put-down	Despairing	Off balance
Judged	Vulnerable	Violated
Devastated	Out of control	Not in control of others
Rejected	Discounted	Abandoned

158

Helpless	Lonely	Disoriented
Dominated	Controlled	Left out
Needy	Shut out	Found out

Do you fear:

Loss of love or relationship	Knowing your partner's deepest
Loss of self	feelings
Loss of face	Knowing yourself
	Intimacy

1. What am I afraid will happen if I open to my pain?

    ___ I'll die.

    ___ I'll go crazy.

    ___ I'll kill myself.

    ___ I'll be weak, a wimp.

    ___ I'll be rejected and be in even more pain.

    ___ I'll lose myself, get taken advantage of, be controlled.

    ___ I'll cry, and it's stupid to cry.

    ___ I'll be in pain forever.

2. What childhood messages and experiences brought about these beliefs?

3. How do I avoid feeling my primary pain?

4. What consequences result from my avoiding pain?

Exercise 24B   Checklist—Self-limiting Beliefs about Pain

___ 1.   No one really wants to hear about my pain.

___ 2.   No one can handle the depth of my pain.

___ 3.   People will think less of me if they see me cry.

___ 4.   If I express my pain, it will be unending.

___ 5.   I can't handle pain.

___ 6.   Showing pain is a sign of weakness.

___ 7.   If I cry, I will be rejected.

___ 8.   If I cry, I will be weak and will fall apart.

___ 9.   Once I start to cry, I'll never stop.

159

___ 10. If I open to my pain, I will go crazy.

___ 11. If I open to my pain, I will die.

___ 12. My problems are so trivial compared to other people's that I have no right to be in pain.

___ 13. I can't handle the pain of rejection.

___ 14. Getting rejected is a pain worse than death.

___ 15. If I open to my pain, people will think I'm crazy.

___ 16. There's no point in opening to pain. It doesn't make anything better.

___ 17. Opening to pain is dumb, a waste of time.

25. TRUE COMMUNICATION

Underneath your protections is your true communication. It's the part of you that would speak with the honesty of a child—the soft, frightened, vulnerable part that just wants to be heard and acknowledged and appreciated but is too afraid to ask for what it needs. It's not your Higher Self, but it is a part of you that opens the doorway to it. It's the lovable part of you that is most often judged as weak, the part you hide for fear that you will be controlled.

Remember a time in your life when you reacted protectively—with anger and/or fear—because someone tried to control you or did something that upset you. Recall a time when you expressed anger to someone you care for. Recall as many of the details as you can: where the situation occurred, what the circumstances were. Feel inside how terrible it felt to get angry, how trapped you felt by your anger, and how frustrated you must have been, not knowing what else to do. And ask yourself: "What was I really feeling under that anger? What did I *really* want to say to that person?" Likely, you wanted to say, "I'm afraid I'll lose you," or, "It scares me when you come home late and I don't know where you are," or, "I get scared that you don't love me when you don't want to touch me."

Look inside and see what you really wanted to say. Stop, close your eyes, and feel what has gone unexpressed far too long.

Feel how much your heart longs to talk to the people you have loved and now love, to tell them what you are really feeling underneath the protections. Feel how good it would be to hold them and let your heart really speak. Now is your chance to do that.

Exercise 25A   Practicing True Communication

1. Think of a conflict in which you reacted by wanting to control another and either write or describe the situation out loud as if the other person were really there with you now.

2. After describing the situation, describe what you really felt and what you really wanted to say.

EXAMPLE: The incident was when I came home very excited from a conference I had attended and my husband was shut down and unresponsive. I became very irritated and angry with him, calling him names and threatening to just not be around him when he was like that.

What I really felt was sad and alone. What I really wanted to say to him was, "When you're unresponsive it really feels awful. I feel as if all the wind is let out of my sails. I feel alone and scared that you don't like who I am. I don't know if it's that you don't like my being so enthusiastic or if what I'm actually saying upsets you. I get so confused and feel tense in my whole body."

3. Remember and write as many incidents as you can and become more and more aware of how you feel under your protections.

4. If you want to share the incidents with the person who was involved, make sure that your intention is to learn more about yourself and the very good reasons the other person had for reacting as he did. If your intention is to get something from the other person or to make him feel guilty and wrong, expect a defensive reaction.

Exercise 25B   Checklist—Self-limiting Beliefs about Listening and Learning

___ 1.   If I really listen and open to learning from another I will lose myself.
___ 2.   If I'm open to listening and learning I will get talked out of my own views and feelings.
___ 3.   If I'm open to listening and learning I will get knocked off my own path.

___ 4. If I'm open to listening and learning I will find out how people really see me and I will end up being the wrong one, the bad guy.

___ 5. If I'm open to listening and learning I will find out that I am unlovable and/or inadequate.

___ 6. If I'm open to listening and learning I will find out that other people think I'm a jerk.

___ 7. If I'm open to listening and learning I will get criticized or blamed for other people's unhappiness and then I will have to change to make them happy.

___ 8. If I listen to someone else, I will never get listened to.

___ 9. If I really listen openly to someone I will hear things that are painful and I won't be able to handle the pain.

26. TELLING AND HEARING THE TRUTH

Telling the truth is one of the most difficult things to do. We continually deny, withhold, or distort the truth because of our fears that others can't handle it, may leave us, emotionally or physically, or that we don't have the right to feel as we do or want what we want.

For example, many people stay in emotionally or physically abusive situations without telling the truth. The truth is, "When you behave this way, I don't like being around you." It may be difficult to realize that when someone is being abusive, the loving behavior is to confront that person and not let him/her believe that the situation is acceptable to you. Instead, we go right to our protections, withdrawing, attempting to placate, or becoming combative.

In what areas are you not being truthful? (Do you make love when you don't want to, or are you cheating on your partner? Do you feel bored with or disrespectful of your partner? Are you feeling taken advantage of by your boss, your employee, or your child?) What are the consequences of not telling the truth? How do you wind up feeling about yourself? What happens between you and the other person?

Not telling the truth guarantees that you and the other person will remain stuck. The truth shakes things up, but it is the only chance that you both have to learn and grow. Speaking the truth is the loving thing to do. Your partner may not respond to your truth as the gift that it is—he or she may be too scared—but you'll never know that until you are honest.

If you approach someone from a place of fear, you likely will receive a defensive reaction. The fact that your own protective barriers are up is reflected in your tone of voice and your body language. If you fear a hostile reaction, you will probably approach defensively. But if you approach the person with softness and openness—open to understanding and accepting the other's reaction and to sharing with him/her your own feelings—you have a much better chance of receiving openness in return.

In the face of your best efforts to remain open and loving, others may still retreat into being self-righteous victims. But what alternatives do you have? If you don't tell them the truth, they may seem happy, but you'll be miserable. You'll feel imprisoned by your relationships and eventually resent the relationships and dislike yourself. Keeping secrets usually injures intimacy. Honesty *is* risky and often leads to problems. But it's necessary if you want better relationships and greater self-esteem.

Hearing the truth is equally difficult. For example, if you want honesty and closeness with your children, you have to be willing to hear that they may be doing things that you consider wrong, like taking drugs or having sex. If you want to know why they lie to you, you have to be willing to hear that maybe they are afraid of your punitive or judgmental reactions. In order to deal effectively with the situation, you have to be open to learning about what you are doing that makes your child afraid of being honest with you.

No one can tell you how much you should say or when to speak the truth about how you feel. One of our favorite sayings is, "All important decisions must be made on the basis of insufficient data." You can never know how another person will react. You can only have faith that whatever happens, you have the power to learn from it and to turn any problem into an opportunity.

Exercise 26A   Practicing Telling and Hearing the Truth

When doing this exercise with a partner, sit facing each other.

Person revealing truth:

"A truth about myself (an action, a feeling, a belief) that I've never told you is. . . ."

Person receiving truth:

1. "What I'd like to explore and understand about your truth is. . . ."

2. "How I'm feeling about what you've told me is. . .."

3. "What I need to explore and understand about my own feelings is. . . ."

If you are working with a person you are in a relationship with, you can use this truth as a basis for exploration.

If you are not working with someone you are in a relationship with, first tell the truth as if the other person is your parent, mate, child, etc.; then explore with your partner your fear and beliefs in telling the truth to that person.

When doing this exercise alone:

1. Complete the following sentence in as much detail as you can: "A truth about myself (an action, a feeling, a belief) that I've never shared with anyone is. . . ."

2. What are the negative consequences of not admitting this truth—the negative effects that it has had on your feelings about yourself, the other person, and on your relationship?

LET GO

To "let go" does not mean to stop caring, it means I can't do it for someone else.

To "let go" is not to cut myself off, it's the realization I can't control another.

To "let go" is not to enable, but allow learning from natural consequences.

To "let go" is to admit powerlessness, which means the outcome is not in my hands.

To "let go" is not to try to change or blame another, it's to make the most of myself.

To "let go" is not to care for, but to care about.

To "let go" is not to fix, but to be supportive.

To "let go" is not to judge, but to allow another to be a human being.

To "let go" is not to be in the middle arranging all the outcomes, but to allow others to affect their destinies.

To "let go" is not to be protective, it's to permit another to face reality.

To "let go" is not to deny, but to accept.

To "let go" is not to nag, scold or argue, but instead to search out my own shortcomings and correct them.

To "let go" is not to adjust everything to my desires but to take each day as it comes and cherish myself in it.

To "let go" is not to criticize or regulate anybody, but to try to become what I dream I can be.

To "let go" is not to regret the past, but to grow and live for the future.

To "let go" is to fear less and love more.

—Anonymous

·8·

HEALING

Emotional abuse—being slighted, criticized, ridiculed, dismissed, rejected—is rampant in most people's relationships and even is thought by some to be helpful and loving.

Abusive experiences are compounded in childhood by either having to hide the hurt and suffer alone or being further abused for showing the hurt. Being told that there is something wrong with you for your reactions ("There, there, it's not so bad"; "I'll give you something to cry about!"; "What's the matter, can't you take a joke?") leaves deep scars. A child's protections are attempts to relieve pain and to avoid it in the future.

As adults, we continue to act out the same patterns. Have you ever berated yourself with variations on the theme, "You're such a jerk, what's wrong with you?" Judgments and disrespect are so ingrained in us that we rarely stop to consider the devastating effects on ourselves and others. Protections are the scars that cover the deep wounds of emotional abuse. Healing those wounds is an important part of becoming open to learning. But the healing can happen only when you stop being a victim.

In chapter 6 we discussed two kinds of pain: blaming, victim pain ("Poor me, you're making me miserable"), which shifts responsibility to others, prevents learning, and keeps the person stuck; and nonblaming pain, in which you feel the sadness appropriate to the situation, accept your responsibility in creating it, and move on to learn about yourself.

For example, people caught up in victim pain blame their parents (and others) for their unhappiness. They don't understand that their parents were doing the best they could—that their parents' actions were the products of their own erroneous beliefs, and thus no one is to blame. The situation is terribly sad, as we all missed out on getting and giving the love we needed in our growing-up years. We have been damaged, and we need to do some repair work, but that work can bring us into a clearer and better place. We can damn our parents (and others), or we can be thankful that we have the capacity to help ourselves. If we're lucky, we have people around us who care enough to help us in our relearning process.

Important healing takes place when you feel compassion for those who have been hurt by your protections, sadness over their being hurt, and forgiveness of yourself and others. Harboring resentment, anger, and blame is not helpful in your healing process. Forgiveness of others releases you from your self-blame, and then your self-esteem rises and you feel less protected and more loving.

27. COMPASSION, SADNESS, AND FORGIVENESS

Compassion is that feeling you get when you understand another person so deeply that you feel as he/she does. You *can* do this, because others feel as you do. The key is to be more in touch with your own feelings. You are blocked from knowing others' feelings primarily when you don't want to know your own. You don't want to know that your criticism, sarcasm, icy withdrawal, raging anger— any behavior that produces guilt or fear in another—is painful to that person. If you faced this, even though you are not responsible for the other's feelings, you would feel bad, and it would be much harder to continue that behavior. You want to be protected, and you believe that your protections don't have an effect. And that's just not true. You also don't want to know how painful another's protections are to you. You want to believe that you can take it, that little things like sarcasms or criticisms or slights don't hurt you. But that's not true either. All of us are very sensitive and have many beliefs that create a great deal of pain, and protecting against this pain affects us all.

It hurts others to be with you when you are protected, even though it is not your fault that they feel that way. As we have said before, whenever a person feels hurt, it is *his* responsibility. Nevertheless, it is *your* responsibility to realize that this person (child, mate, employee, parent) has fears and beliefs and that your protections are painful to him.

Sadness is the feeling that occurs when, without blaming yourself or others, you realize the mess your protections have created. To feel sad without feeling guilty or wrong is not easy, but it is possible and necessary if you are to move forward. You protect when you feel wrong and/or guilty and that keeps you from feeling the vulnerable feeling of sadness. Without accepting and feeling that sadness, you can't move on to the next step, which is forgiveness.

Forgiveness occurs naturally when you feel nonblaming sadness. There is, in fact, no one to blame. We all act from a great deal of ignorance and from the fears that our erroneous beliefs have created. We are not mean, malicious people, but when frightened, we behave exactly as we have sworn not to. Forgiveness is what allows you to behave with true compassion and love, to become the loving person that you inherently are. It is through spreading this love that our planet can be healed.

As generally understood, forgiveness is a process in which I forgive you for being wrong. This is a subtle form of condescension, attack and manipulation. Therefore, popular as it is, it is not forgiveness. True forgiveness is the awareness that what we perceive as attacks are not what they seem to be. They are statements of fear or pain and are actually distorted calls for love. Anytime I feel that I'm being attacked, I have forgotten the true underlying message, probably because my own wounds and self-limiting beliefs are making it difficult to remember. But once I become an adult, you can never truly attack me emotionally, spiritually or psychologically, you can only reactivate the fear and pain already within me from having been abused as a child. And therefore the process of true forgiveness entails the recognition that if you never attacked me, there is nothing I need to forgive you for. How could I forgive you for having emotional wounds, for being afraid, for feeling guilty, for being in pain? What is there to forgive?

If you were physically and/or emotionally abused as a child, forgiving your parents may or may not be important to you. If it helps you to move on in your own healing, then this is important. But sometimes forgiveness cuts off the healing by short-circuiting the anger and rage that needs to be released to heal. For adult survivors of childhood abuse, forgiveness may eventually happen, but should never be forced or expected.

True forgiveness is a paradox. The acknowledgment that there is nothing to forgive another for is precisely what true forgiveness is.

Following is an exercise that will help you let go of blame and feel your compassion and forgiveness for yourself and others. There are three parts to the exercise, and it will take about an hour.

Part 1 is designed to increase your understanding of what another person really feels. You will name the person you believe has been hurt as a result of your protections; then you "become" that person, by talking as he/she would. First, complete the sentences: "Someone who has been hurt by my (name your protection) is (fill in the person's name). Now I'm going to become (say the person's name again)." Then speak as that person would, feeling what it is like to be at the other end of your protections. Keep your eyes closed to enhance your feelings of actually becoming the other person. Read the following demonstrations and the visualization before you do part 1. We suggest that you spend at least fifteen minutes on part 1. Then proceed to part 2 for five to ten minutes, and read part 3.

Demonstrations: One Person Doing the Exercise Alone

JORDAN: Someone I've hurt with my icy withdrawal is my son Eric. Now I'm going to become Eric.

(*As Eric*): Dad, when I do something that you don't like and you get silent, I really get scared. I'm so afraid to do anything that upsets you because I don't want you to be angry with me. I feel awful when you withdraw. I get scared that you won't love me unless I'm exactly what you think I should be. I feel as if I have no room to be me, to mess up. I really want you to love me, and I really try. Please love me.

Repeat this process with everyone you have hurt with your protections.

Two People Doing the Exercise Together

Alternate one person at a time, as illustrated below. For example: Margie identifies one of her protections and the person who was hurt; she then becomes that person. Next, Jordan identifies one of his protections and the person who was hurt and he becomes that person. Then it goes back to Margie for a second turn, then Jordan takes a second turn, and so on.

The demonstration shows one cycle, but you will do as many as you can in fifteen minutes.

MARGIE: Someone I've hurt by being irritated and parental is my husband, Jordan. Now I'm going to become Jordan.

(*As Jordan*): Margie, when you get that parental, irritated quality, that hard edge in your voice, it feels like you're telling me that I've done it wrong, and that's one of the worst feelings. It feels like you think I don't care about you. And that makes me feel really awful, because I know how much I love you, how important you are to me, and how hard I try to let you know that. When you have that quality in your voice, I feel unseen. I know I get uptight, but what I'm feeling inside is a deep pain in my stomach, because it feels like you just don't see how much I love you.

JORDAN: The person I've hurt with my defensiveness and my closedness to learning is my wife, Margie. Now I'll become Margie.

(*As Margie*): Jordan, you know that the most important thing to me is learning about things. What I've always wanted is for people to want to learn about themselves and me as much as I want to learn about them and myself. And what I really feel sad about is all the opportunities that we've missed to create a wonderful intimacy because you've been threatened by what I wanted to do or what I was thinking about. I feel sad that we haven't created together what I know is possible for us. I'm sad that I haven't had someone there for me the way I know I can be there for others. It leaves me feeling so empty sometimes, shut out, and sad that we haven't created that intimacy.

Visualization—Compassion and Empathy

The following visualization will help you get in touch with your feeling before doing Part 1.

Choose a quiet, comfortable place. Read the visualization silently, slowly allowing the words to sink in and the feelings to flow. (If you are doing this with a partner, one of you will probably finish reading first. Remember, this isn't a competition. Whoever finishes first should continue recalling incidents and feelings until the other partner is ready.)

Take some deep breaths and just relax. . . . Let your awareness go inside. Go back in your memory and recall a time when you hurt someone you loved . . . you hurt him/her very much. Maybe you didn't mean to, but you did. . . . You pushed him/her away, or you said angry words, or you put up a wall between you. Where were you? Who else was around? Imagine how that person must have felt. . . . Let yourself feel his/her feelings for a moment. . . . Did he/she feel afraid of you? Abandoned by you? Brokenhearted? If he/she could have talked to you, what would he/she have said? Open your heart and feel that person's feelings. Don't be afraid of the pain, just feel it. Let down the walls between yourself and that person and feel. Stop, close your eyes, and give yourself time to remember and feel.

Now, take a deep breath and remember a time in your life when you hurt one of your parents. How old were you? Maybe you called your mother names, or maybe you pushed her away or ignored her. Maybe you didn't call your father or visit him, and he felt hurt, even if he didn't show it. Let yourself feel how your parent must have felt . . . like a failure, or sad, or angry. What would he/ she have wanted to say to you? Allow yourself to feel the pain in your parent's heart. . . . Stop, close your eyes, and let the images come.

Now, remember a more recent time in your life when you hurt someone you loved. Maybe you put up a wall between you, and he/ she felt abandoned. . . . Maybe you yelled at him/her . . . rejected him/her sexually . . . left him/her for someone else . . . refused to comfort him/her. . . . Allow yourself to feel how that person felt in his/her heart . . . all the pain, the hurt. . . . Stop, close your eyes, and feel.

And now do Part 1.

Exercise 27A Practicing Forgiveness

Part 1

1. Begin by saying, "Someone I've hurt with my (name the protection) is (name the person)."

2. Become that person and say, "Now I'm going to become—" and feel yourself enter that person's heart; feel yourself inside of him or her and imagine that you are sitting across from yourself.

3. Speaking as the person you've named, tell yourself how hurt you are and what you really wanted.

4. Continue this process for fifteen minutes, using as many people as you can think of.

(If you're doing this with a partner, your partner will do the same thing, and you will go back and forth for fifteen minutes.) Go as deep as you can, with your eyes closed.

Part 2

1. Become yourself again and speak to each of the people whom you have just become, telling them your feelings about having hurt them.

EXAMPLE: "Eric, I feel awful for the many times I hurt you. I know you try hard. I'm sorry that I act that way toward you when I get upset. I know how tense and awful it has made you feel. I really want to have a better relationship with you and I know the tension between us gets in the way. I love you, son."

(If you're doing this with a partner, alternately speak to each of the people you have just become, telling them your feelings about having hurt them.)

2. Continue this process for five to ten minutes, with all the people you named in part 1.

Part 3

Read out loud the following:

"As I look back on all the times I hurt people I loved, I know that I was scared of getting hurt and all I was doing was protecting myself. I never meant to hurt those people, and I know I had good reasons for doing what I did. I know that all I wanted was to be loved and understood, and that I am not bad, just frightened."

Now place your hands over your heart and say the following:

"I forgive myself for all the pain and hurt I have caused others. I release myself from any ways I have been punishing myself. I understand how frightened and protected I was, and I forgive myself and I love myself."

Breathe in that forgiveness and feel it healing you inside and filling you with peace.

And now think about all the people who have hurt you, and say the following:

"I see how everyone who has hurt me never meant to hurt me, just as I never meant to hurt others. I see how scared and protected they were, and that all they wanted was love, too. I can see that the little child was in my parents as well—the little child who didn't get the love he or she wanted growing up, and who got frightened and cold and then couldn't give me the love I needed. Mom and Dad, I understand that you weren't loved the way you needed to be, either, and I forgive you for not always knowing how to love me in the way I needed. I forgive you for hurting me. And I forgive myself for hurting you. And I feel the forgiveness connecting me to you, wherever you are, and giving me peace. And I can now understand the unloved little child within my lovers or partners and see how they didn't mean to hurt me either, but they too were unloved and afraid. And I forgive them in my heart for hurting me. And as I think about all of us on this planet, and how frightened we are inside, and how we protect ourselves from being hurt again, and end up hurting others, I send a shower of forgiveness to all of humanity for being so scared, and for putting up the walls we do. I feel my commitment to love rather than to those walls, and to compassion rather than protection."

Discussion from the Workshop

SHARING: I was surprised at the depth of the sadness. But it wasn't inexhaustible. There was a limit. I can let it go. What a relief!

SHARING: I don't understand how I could feel such deep pain and have it be a really wonderful experience. It actually felt good. I don't understand how pain can at one time feel good and at other times it's awful.

MARGIE: The pain of the victim is a very helpless, terrible pain to feel. But the pain of cleansing, which this is, is very releasing, very healing when you go into it.

SHARING: The pain feels like it's moving out. Is it?

JORDAN: Yes, because you are releasing something from within you. It's like a festering wound inside, and there is a healing when you move that out. The other pain—victim pain—never feels good.

SHARING: Now I know why I've come back here three times—the specialness of learning to love myself, and to put myself into the other person and experience within me what that person felt like when I hurt him. I think that being able to experience myself through the eyes of the other person is the most powerful exercise of all.

SHARING: I'm not quite sure what my fear was, but I couldn't do this exercise. I felt as if I had to have the other person here with me. I have some kind of block on trying to be somebody else.

MARGIE: If you are afraid to feel what another person is feeling, it may be because you are afraid of acknowledging the consequences of your own behavior. That could be an important exploration for you.

SHARING: I had trouble with this exercise because I felt like I had to have a boyfriend or a husband in order to do it.

MARGIE: That may be one of your limiting beliefs, because you've lived your whole life with relationships. If you believe that the only time you can feel compassion and empathy is with a mate, that would be very limiting for you.

SHARING: I saw that the most important thing I need is to forgive myself. Pain, fear, anger—they all wash away in that forgiveness. Thank you.

SHARING: I was finally able to say good-bye to my mother, who died three years ago.

JORDAN: So the forgiveness—and I think this is true for all of us—is really for us. It is freeing. People are afraid to forgive for fear that it will let the other person off the hook, that they are really giving in. They think they are too hurt to be able to forgive the person who "did it" to them. If you're having trouble letting go of something, there is a good reason why you're hanging on to it. But it's important to know that letting go of it is not for them. It's for *you*.

Exercise 27B   Checklist—Self-limiting Beliefs about Forgiveness

___ 1.   I need to continue to punish myself so that those I've hurt will suffer less.

___ 2.   I need to punish myself to make sure that I don't keep doing the things that hurt myself and others.

___ 3.   If I forgive my parents, I will be too vulnerable and I will get hurt again.

___ 4.   If I forgive my partner, he/she will never change.

___ 5.   Forgiving myself is selfish and self-indulgent.

___ 6.   Once I'm forgiven, then I'm absolved and I can protect again.

___ 7.   If I forgive the people who hurt me, they will just keep hurting me.

___ 8.   Forgiving myself and others makes me weak.

___ 9.   I don't deserve to be forgiven.

28.   CHILDHOOD PAIN

To relive your childhood pain and finally finish with it, we suggest that you choose someone to work with you, either someone who loves you or a caring therapist. Pain can be healed in the presence of love. Experiencing deep pain alone is not advisable for most people because it merely replays the original incident. The painful events of your childhood, from minor disappointments and rejections to tragedies such as the death of a parent or your parents' divorce, would not have caused you such trauma if you had experienced your deep pain in the presence of love and been allowed to continue feeling your feelings until you were through with them. The mourning period varies for each person, but eventually the pain would have healed, you would have learned what you needed to learn from the situation, and you would have been done with it. Instead, most of us carry around deep pockets of pain that we have covered over and now must protect because of our fear of reexperiencing them.

Helping others in pain requires that you allow them to experience the depth of their pain while letting them know that you care about them. There are two ways to approach people when they are in pain. One way communicates your discomfort with pain and your desire to make it go away. The message communicated verbally or nonverbally is, "There, there, everything will be all right. Why don't you think of other things, happy things.'' The other communicates that you have faith that the person has within himself the ability to feel deeply, learn from his pain, and heal himself.

In order to help another, you may have to clear up your own beliefs about pain and about the needs of others when they are in pain. You must believe that people don't need to have their pain "made better" or their problems solved. You are not responsible for fixing anybody else's pain. All you need to do is be there to listen to, care about, and respect that person's feelings.

Exercise 28A   Healing Childhood Pain

Tell your partner exactly what you need him/her to do for you to feel cared for—how you need to be held or touched, what you need him/her to say or not to say, how you can best be comforted. You may also want to have a soft object to rub on your lips or face or a stuffed animal to hold on to. Anything that you need for your nurturing is okay.

1. Recall a painful incident from your childhood and say, "A time I felt hurt growing up was. . . ."

2. Now say, "What I really wanted to say was. . . ."

EXAMPLE: A time I felt hurt growing up was when my parents left our farm in upstate New York to move to California, and I knew I wasn't going to see my grandfather again. What I really wanted to say was, "Grandpa is the only person who loves me. I don't want to leave him. Please don't take me away. I love you, Grandpa. I don't think I can live without you."

3. Let yourself sink deeply into your feelings and allow yourself to be healed with the love your partner is giving you.

Doing this exercise over and over again with the same or different issues in the presence of love will heal it and you will no longer have to protect against it.

Following is a long visualization to help you bring deep feelings to the surface.

Create a peaceful environment in which you can relax and feel safe; a quiet space with dim lighting is usually helpful. If music is on, make sure it is quiet and restful. Your partner will read the visualization slowly, taking time to allow your mind to drift back in time. The visualization will assist you in completing the above exercise.

Visualization—The Child Within

Begin by taking some nice, deep, relaxing breaths, right in the middle of your chest, and when you exhale, let all the tension go as you breathe out. If you are aware of any places in your body that are tense, breathe into those places. Relax and allow yourself to travel back now, back as far as you can remember, back to a time when you were very small, a little girl or a little boy. Feel yourself turning back into that child right now. Remember how you looked, and picture yourself looking that way. What was your favorite toy? Who were your friends? Just let your mind go, and feel that little child stirring inside you. Now, remember a time in your childhood when something happened that hurt you . . . something or someone hurt you . . . and re-create that time in your mind. Remember where you were, what was happening . . . who was with you . . . how you were feeling inside. Find that feeling right now, because it is still buried inside your heart, and it's been there for a long, long time. . . . Just breathe into it. . . . Take a moment to remember.

What happened that hurt you so much? Did someone say something mean to you? Hit you? Ignore you, or act cold toward only you? Did someone leave you? Disappoint you? Did you lose something? Go back and feel how betrayed you felt, feel how much it hurt you so deep inside. . . . Think about how it was.

What did you want to say to that person who hurt you? What did you really want? And whom did you want to ask for what you wanted?. . . Maybe you wanted to say, "Mommy, please don't tell me I'm bad . . . please be proud of me and love me . . .," or maybe you wanted to say, "Daddy, please don't go away and leave us all alone. Please don't leave me, Daddy!" Tell yourself that it is all right for you to feel all those feelings again. . . . Remember how scared you were. . . .

179

Remember what you did when you were hurt. Did you hide in your room and cry? Curl up under the covers where no one could find you? Run to a brother or sister to be comforted? Did you hide the feelings inside? Did you get angry and throw a temper tantrum? Feel all those hurts now, all that pain from long ago, every time you felt unloved, unappreciated, frightened, neglected, misunderstood, lonely, or angry. Feel the place inside where that hurt child still lives, hiding behind your protective walls because you don't want to feel any more pain, you don't want to be hurt anymore. Feel that hurt place inside of you. . . .

What did you need to feel better when you felt so hurt? What did you need when you were frightened or in pain? Did you want your daddy to come and hold you in his arms and tell you he understood your pain and would protect you? Did you want your mommy to be there to kiss you, listen to your pain, and tell you everything would be all right? Did you want someone to promise you he wouldn't hurt you anymore? Feel how much you just wanted someone to understand your pain, how much you just wanted someone to be there to hold you and make it better . . . and how scared you were that no one would ever make it better for you, no one would ever really understand how much you hurt . . . no one would ever love you the way you wanted to be loved. . . . Remember how it felt. . . .

Now, reach out and take my hands. . . . This is a time to let that little child out, to let go of the pain you've been carrying around for so long, to let the pain out and let it be healed by the love I will give you. . . . I want you to imagine that the person who hurt you is sitting in front of you . . . and I want you to ask that person for what you really wanted. Imagine you are talking right to that person. You will be saying, "A time I felt hurt growing up was . . ." and, "What I really wanted to say was. . . ." And I will be here to listen and love you silently. Take five to ten minutes to pour out as many incidents as you can remember. Begin now.

After completing this part of the visualization, take a few moments to relax, then close your eyes again and listen to your partner read the following:

Take a big deep breath into your heart, feel all that pain releasing, feel all the walls tumbling down—and feel inside of you whatever your child needs to feel better. . . . What does he(she) need to hear? How does he need to be held? Ask your child what he needs now . . . and this is a beautiful opportunity for you to give that child the love and comfort he has always wanted. Feel that child inside of you, and reach out and ask me for what you want . . . how you want to be loved and comforted. Imagine I am all the people who hurt you, all the people you needed love from who didn't give it to you. . . . Just let the little child pour his heart out and say, "Please don't leave me, please love me, I need you so much, I get so afraid. . . ." Whatever you want to say. . . . Just let the little child cry and talk, and I'm going to reach out and hold that little child as if he were my own, and comfort him and love him and say all the things he needs to hear, and just let my love heal it, shower him with love and make him feel safe again. Let your child just collapse into feeling all the hurt, and I will be here to give him all the love he ever wanted.

When you are finished, thank your partner, then switch roles so that he/she has a chance to be the little child and to reach out for healing, while you become the loving comforter.

Afterward, thank each other and spend some time together sharing your healing.

29. SELF-FORGIVENESS AND SELF-LOVE

The following visualization should be used anytime you are judging or blaming yourself. Read it, have someone read it to you—even better—make a tape for yourself.

Relax and close your eyes. Take some deep breaths and let them out with a sigh. Shake out any tension in your body and just relax. Relax. Allow your mind to drift back in time . . . and let your

181

memories go back to a time when you were very young. Begin to see a movie of your life going backward . . . back . . . back . . . to a time when you were very hurt. Maybe your mother or father yelled at you or ridiculed you, laughed at you or hit you. And you had no one to go to for comfort. And remember a time when you were upset, when you were crying, when you were alone and there was no one to comfort you. See yourself alone in your bedroom. . . . See your shoes and the kind of clothes you wore. . . . See yourself as you were: see how small you were, how soft you were. And feel how sad you were and how alone and how scared. . . . And feel how overwhelming all those feelings felt in your young, tender body. Just feel how all alone you were.

And now, imagine yourself, as you are now, quietly going into the room where your little girl or boy is. . . . Take a moment to see yourself crying, all alone . . . maybe thinking that it's all your fault . . . or that nobody cares . . . or that you're going to die. . . . Now, as your adult self, go over to your little self and take him (her) in your arms and tell him who you are and that it's going to be all right . . . that you survived this pain and lived . . . and that you've come back to comfort him. Put your little self on your adult lap, hold him close to you, and use all of your adult resources to comfort him. Feel how warm he is, feel the softness of the skin on his little face as you brush the tears away, feel the soft silkiness of his hair as you stroke it and murmur soft words of love. Feel how tightly he holds you and how he gradually relaxes and stops crying and starts to open to your healing love. . . . Tell your little self that you'll never have to hurt in solitude and loneliness again, that you will take care of yourself and love yourself whenever that little child needs you in the future.

When you feel ready, take that little child and actually pull him inside of you. . . . Feel him enter your body. That little child is a part of you, a spontaneous and energetic part of your life. Take in the aliveness, the curiosity, the creativity, the sense of wonder of your little child. Feel that energy within you and know that you will be able to share it with your inner child. Just sit for a moment and relax and enjoy what you're feeling. Remember how intense you

were, how full of life, how interested and curious and loving . . .
how life was full of wonder. . . . Let those feelings spread throughout
your body. . . . When you're ready, open your eyes and come back
to the now.

Inflicting pain on yourself through self-judgment or self-blame
is not loving behavior. Next time you hurt or are angry with yourself
or are in any way judging yourself, try loving yourself instead.
Remember that you had good, important reasons for developing your
protections. If you can take that crucial step of loving yourself for
whatever you hate about yourself, you will open the door to seeing
the erroneous beliefs that underlie your protections. Your little child
needed and deserved to be understood and loved. . .and so do you.

Now it's your responsibility to learn how to be a loving parent
to your inner child, to overcome your own unlovingness to yourself.
If You Really Loved Me was written to describe what it means to be a
loving parent, but also has proven extremely valuable to learn what it
means to be loving to your inner child.

The Way of Transformation

The man who, being really on the Way, falls upon hard times in the world will not, as a consequence, turn to that friend who offers him refuge and comfort and encourages his old self to survive. Rather, he will seek out someone who will faithfully and inexorably help him to risk himself, so that he may endure the suffering and pass courageously through it, thus making of it a "raft that leads to the far shore." Only to the extent that man exposes himself over and over again to annihilation, can that which is indestructible arise within him. In this lies the dignity of daring. Thus, the aim of practice is not to develop an attitude which allows a man to acquire a state of harmony and peace wherein nothing can ever trouble him. On the contrary, practice should teach him to let himself be assaulted, perturbed, moved, insulted, broken and battered—that is to say, it should enable him to dare to let go his futile hankering after harmony, surcease from pain, and a comfortable life in order that he may discover, in doing battle with the forces that oppose him, that which awaits him beyond the world of opposites. The first necessity is that we should have the courage to face life, and to encounter all that is most perilous in the world. Only if we venture repeatedly through zones of annihilation can our contact with Divine Being, which is beyond annihilation, become firm and stable. The more a man learns whole-heartedly to confront the world that threatens him with isolation, the more are the depths of the Ground of Being revealed and the possibilities of new life and Becoming opened.

—Karlfried Gräf von Durckheim,
The Way of Transformation

· 9 ·

CONTINUING THE PROCESS

Becoming a more loving person is a lifelong process. It is an ideal that you can always move closer to. It doesn't matter where you start or where you end. The only thing that's important is that you're in the process.

You can look forward to your life and relationships improving as you become more loving. There probably won't be any drastic, sudden changes, although that is possible. Changes usually occur slowly, with plenty of ups and downs. Your ego will fight the changes tooth and nail, and your ego is very powerful. You will have to be fully, consciously dedicated to this process if you are to be successful at it.

Dedication means using the formats for learning (chapter 4) over and over again. It means continuing to make your personal growth and learning a high priority. It means remembering that everything in your life is an opportunity to learn and to be grateful. Tuning in to what others have found in their journeys can also assist in your learning process, so we've included a recommended-reading list.

Connecting with like-minded people is very important. Any group that fosters personal responsibility and spirituality would most likely be supportive. Or you could form your own support group of people trying to put into practice the principles of loving behavior. A support group could be just you and one other person, or more people if you wish. Exercise 33 contains a few suggestions on how to get a group started.

Doing the exercises and discussing the ideas presented in this book with a close friend will deepen your learning. Remember, this is a spiritual, psychological, and emotional journey. And the only person who has all the answers for you is *you*. Inside you lies the truth.

Avoid those who want only to indoctrinate you into their truth. Surround yourself with people whose intention is to help you find your truth while they're finding theirs.

The four ways of working together that follow will be helpful in your ongoing and deepening understanding of this material when you're working with other people.

30. BEING A HELPER

When you are helping another person explore, your goal is to guide the person to understand and learn from his/her feelings and behavior, become aware of his/her protections and the beliefs and fears behind them, and assume personal responsibility for his/her own learning.

To help people who are in the process of exploring their feelings, you must be with them totally, not thinking about your own views on the subject or about what you will say next. It's not a conversation. You must be interested and caring enough to feel their feelings and to offer them loving support when they get in touch with their pain and tears.

Your job is to help them find their self-limiting beliefs. Your comments and questions should help the explorer to stay focused and go deeper into his/her feelings, to help him/her differentiate between thinking and feeling. Awarenesses that come out of a feeling experience are usually more meaningful. You should also point out any significant body language, such as tension in the posture, a sad look in the eyes, or a frightened look on the face. For the most part, you will stay in the moment, focusing on the explorer's protections rather than his/her story.

Examples of helpful questions:

- What are you feeling right now?
- What do you want right now?
- What do you want to learn about right now?
- What do you think your intention is right now?
- What do you think are the important reasons you have for feeling this way?

188

- What are you unhappy about?
- Why does that make you feel unhappy?
- What are you doing that keeps you from getting what you want?
- What is the belief behind your feeling?
- Where did you get that belief?
- Why do you believe that?
- Is it accurate?

When you find it difficult to put aside your own fears and beliefs in order to give genuine caring and interest to help another person, you need to stop and explore your own fears and protections. This will make you a more helpful facilitator.

31. OBSERVING AS A THIRD PARTY

In this mode, three people work together in the exploration process. While the helper is working with the explorer, the third person acts as an observer.

The observer's job is to keep the helper on a learning track so that he/she doesn't slip into being a caretaker, and to point out when either the helper or the explorer lapses into protections.

What to look for:

Explanations
Accusations, blaming
Rationalizations
Excuses
Attacks
Defenses
Criticisms
Analysis
Problem-solving
Making others responsible, wrong
Being helpless, a victim, not taking responsibility
Not wanting to learn about self

As an observer, you must be attuned to your feelings. When you feel uncomfortable, anxious, or defensive, chances are the interaction you are observing has left the learning track. Your inner tension alerts you to another's protections as well as your own.

Your task is not to judge, analyze, or problem-solve, but merely to gently point out your observations or ask questions only to the helper.

Examples of helpful interventions:

- Are you feeling attacked right now? I'm feeling uncomfortable. I've got a weight in the pit of my stomach, which I usually get when I feel blamed. What are you feeling?
- You seem to be "leading the witness." Are you having difficulty staying with him/her?
- The interaction seems to have deteriorated into defensiveness. How are you feeling about it?
- You seem to be giving the explorer advice. Why would you rather problem-solve?

32. TWO COUPLES HELPING EACH OTHER

A fascinating learning experience occurs when two couples work together as in the following exploration process.

1. Each person partners with the person of the opposite sex in the other couple.

2. One set of partners is designated as the participant, while the other set is the silent observer.

3. Each person in the participating set chooses something he/she would like to learn about, then each takes five minutes to be an explorer and five minutes to be a helper.

4. The two sets of partners switch roles, so that the observers become participants and vice versa. In addition to whatever learning takes place during the exploration, this exercise provides a wonderful opportunity for each person to become aware of how different he/she is with another person. The participants may find themselves having a much easier time than they would have with their own partners. The observers may see their mates in an entirely different light. Reactions like "I never believed he could be so open" are not uncommon.

5. Noting the differences can then lead into discussions: "Why are we different with others? What is it in our interactions that produces the deadness, the defensiveness, etc.?" Each person has the opportunity to learn about his/her part of the system.

33. SUPPORT GROUPS

One of the most exciting and valuable learning experiences occurs when like-minded people get together to share their process.

A support group is a good place to turn when you get stuck—and you will get stuck. The ideas presented in this book are so different from your previous programming that doubts, questions, and difficulties will arise, and at that point many people may feel tempted to give up. In a support group, you'll get additional input that may free your thinking.

In a support group, you will also share your "highs." Hearing about the successes of others provides an important motivation to continue with your learning, and you may also get some new ideas as to where you are stuck. If you find you are judging yourself for not being "further ahead," that gives you another wonderful opportunity to learn about your self-limiting beliefs.

The purpose of the group is not to offer therapy or to tell people what to do, but to find ways to grow and to practice the intention to learn. The focus should be on finding the loving (caring) behavior in a conflict and discovering the fears and beliefs that are blocking that behavior.

We have found that leaderless groups don't work very well unless they are structured, so we strongly recommend that you follow as closely as possible the structure outlined below.

Structure of the Meetings

Part 1   (20 minutes)—Sharing

This is a time for group members to share both their excitement and their frustrations, the positive things that are happening as a result of becoming more loving and the difficulties they are experiencing.

Part 2   (20 minutes)—Discuss Reading

Each week, read aloud from *From Conflict to Caring* and discuss the material. The following are typical assignments: Meeting 1, pages 14-18; Meeting 2, pages 18-22; Meeting 3, pages 22-26; etc.

Part 3   (10 minutes)—Meditation

Do a centering exercise. This might be just a deep breathing meditation or listening to any centering tape that a member has found helpful.

Part 4   (50 minutes)—Finding the Loving Behavior

    A. (20 minutes)—Complete the following format:

        1. What was the conflict?

        2. Describe your reaction.

        3. If your reaction did not leave you feeling peaceful and enhance your self-esteem, you know it was not a loving response. What were the results of your behavior:

            a. Between you and the other person?

            b. To yourself?

        4. What would a loving response be? What response would promote personal responsibility and enhance your self-esteem?

        5. What fears and beliefs would stop you from this behavior?

    B. (10 minutes)—Find a partner and take five minutes each to help each other with questions 4 and 5.

    C. (20 minutes)—Get back together as a group and help anyone who requests help in deepening his/her understanding of questions 4 and 5.

Part 5   (20 minutes)—Social Time!

Enjoy one another and use any conflicts that arise interpersonally as opportunities to use the Formats for Learning.

Setting Up a Group

The group should consist of six to ten members. Meetings can be held at someone's home, and the responsibility of refreshments (if the group decides to have them) can be shared or rotated. Meeting from 7:30 to 9:30 P.M. every two weeks, on a weeknight, seems to work out well, although each group will find its own best schedule. Discuss schedules well in advance, taking into account vacations, trips, and holidays.

One member should assume the role of leader. The leadership can be changed periodically to give other members the opportunity for leadership experience. The leader takes the responsibility to schedule and organize the meetings. Initially he/she will make up a group roster and have copies available at the meeting. Any cost incurred by the leader should be shared by the group.

Generally, the role of the leader is to see that the group sticks to its schedule. It is important to remember that this is *not* group therapy! Each member should be encouraged to take responsibility for his/her own learning and to inform the group of his/her needs or feelings about the group. The leader should be prepared to deal with any serious conflicts, unresolved issues, or philosophical questions and not allow them to sidetrack meetings.

How to Find People

Finding like-minded people requires first your intention to do so. Then turn your attention to connecting with people who are familiar with our books. The following suggestions are only a few of the many possibilities:

1. Check with your local bookstores; they may be able to help you contact people who have expressed interest in our work.

2. Put up notices in places that might attract people who are interested in learning about themselves—for example, churches, healing centers, and libraries.

As you find other ways that work for you, we'd appreciate your sharing them with us.

34. THE LEARNING LOG

The Learning Log can be photocopied and used to keep track of and focus on your learning.

ISSUE EXPLORED: DATE:

PROTECTIONS EXPLORED:

1. New understandings I gained about my beliefs concerning:

The issue:

My protections:

2. What have I learned about how to get out of my protected position?

3. How do I feel about myself right now and what has led to these feelings?

4. What do I need to learn more about?

35. DEEPENING INTIMACY

One of the most important long-term results for couples who use our approach to conflict resolution is ever-deepening intimacy. This has been dramatically demonstrated in the relationships of many couples who have participated in our fourteen-hour Intention Training workshop. We have trained a talented couple, Drs. David and Rebecca Grudermeyer, to conduct the workshop. David and Rebecca have used the Intention Training model in their relationship the entire time they have been together. The intimacy they have achieved is amazing and inspiring, yet well within the grasp of any couple who dedicate themselves to being open to learning. We thought you'd enjoy reading about the experiences of people who have used the path to intimacy and loving behavior for a long time. Now we'll let David and Rebecca speak for themselves.

DAVID &
REBECCA: It's important to keep in mind that one doesn't just snap one's fingers and suddenly become capable of dealing with conflicts fully, gracefully, and rapidly. In fact, when only one of the two people is willing or able to be open, there are differences in the process and in what the loving behavior will end up being. It has taken us years to get to the point where our conflicts are as smooth as they are now. Our relationship is not magical. It is by no means conflict free. It is simply one in which the principle of being open to learning is practiced in an ongoing manner, as a way of life.

To illustrate the process we use, we've chosen a recent, juicy conflict we had at the dinner table.

REBECCA: It was Sunday and David had spent the entire day on the computer. It didn't seem fair to me that he was spending so much time with an inanimate object. I wanted to spend some time with him so I decided to prepare a nice meal for us to have together. Knowing that David had very decided food preferences, I picked a recipe I thought he'd enjoy. I went shopping, set the table with our nice dishes, and spent the better part of the afternoon in the kitchen.

I called David to the table, eagerly anticipating his reaction of undying gratitude to me for working so hard on such a great meal. He took a bite and looked like he was about to choke. He smiled weakly and said something about trying to like it. The look on his face told me that this was a man who really hated this meal. And at that moment, I hated him. How dare he not eat what I had so carefully prepared! I wanted to hit him or shove his face into the plate and make him eat it. My anger was all I felt. I said, "At least you could pretend to like it. You don't have to be such an ass about it."

I knew if I stayed in the same room with David I would say and do things in anger I would later regret, so we separated and I stayed in the kitchen to clean up and mentally enumerate my husband's character defects.

A little voice inside me whispered, "You know this must have something to do with you. It's not all David's fault. What is the pain under your anger?"

At that moment I hated that voice too. I didn't want to give up being right. I But I couldn't both blame David and be happy. I had to give up being the martyr if I wanted to feel better.

As I put the dishes in the sink, I prayed to be willing to explore what was going on. I suddenly felt myself becoming very small. I remembered being eight years old and having prepared a meal with my little sister. It had been horrendous. Our father expected us to do all the meal preparation and he let us know with his subtle but unmistakable look of disapproval that whatever we had prepared was not up to his standard of excellence.

My mother suffered from crippling depression and was simply unable to care for the family. As the oldest child, I felt completely responsible for taking care of the family and pleasing my dad. His look of disapproval filled me with shame—I had failed. I didn't know that I was in an impossible situation and there was no way for me to feel good about myself. I wasn't able to say, "This meal is too much for me, teach me, get some help, but don't expect me to do this, I'm just a little girl."

197

When I realized that this was the reason I had gotten angry at David—that the little girl inside me had reacted when he hadn't liked what I made for dinner—tears began to stream down my face. My anger dissolved almost immediately. My tears cleansed me and helped me release some of the sadness and pain of that ancient wound. I wanted to talk to David about what I had just realized and apologize for blowing up at him.

DAVID: Meanwhile, I had forced down as much of the meal as I could. Offering only icy silence outwardly, I inwardly snarled, "I have given up my whole afternoon laboring on the computer. Doesn't she care that I did it for *us*?! That selfish, ungrateful bitch. She goes and prepares dinner without even checking with me. Something she knows I'll have a hard time eating. And then when I succeeded at curbing my urge to gag and actually ate some of the dinner, she has the nerve to tell me *I'm* the ungrateful one!"

Over the course of what felt like an hour, but in clock time was actually only three or four minutes, I nursed my grievances against her. But soon I started to run out of things to accuse Rebecca of and got tired of feeling victimized. My resentment, anger, and indignation gradually gave way to sadness. I felt propelled back to the circumstances that had led to my being unable to eat some foods without gagging: at my parents' dinner table when I was in elementary school, my mother would passive-aggressively fume at my father, who, to avoid facing her, would cross-examine my brother and me about what had happened at school that day. But school was hell for me. I didn't get very good grades and was bullied a lot. So the last thing in the world I wanted to talk about was school.

I could see myself as a child, sitting there at the dinner table, feeling pain and fear and anger. And I could hear myself making a child's decision: maybe if I choked on my food, my mother would stop scowling and my father would stop cross-examining.

Gagging on foods I didn't like became an automatic habit over time, an involuntary reflex. To this day, anytime I encounter a food I even suspect I might not like, it takes all the self-control I have to suppress the urge to gag. As I reflected on this, sitting alone by myself with my wife that I love a couple of rooms away, I began to cry. I felt so foolish. I realized that my anger toward Rebecca had been a replay of the past and had *nothing* to do with her or the meal. My spontaneous desire was to apologize to Rebecca and tell her the way I felt about the flashback I had had, and also to apologize to my inner child for initially ignoring the pain and fear he was feeling.

DAVID &
REBECCA: When we came back together, we had both been crying. Because the anger in both of us was gone, we were able to sit down tenderly with each other and share the fact that both of us had gotten directly in touch with an old wound through our explorations. We talked until we both fully, empathically, and nonjudgmentally appreciated the momentary nightmare the other person had felt ensnared in.

David acknowledged that his part in the conflict was that he became so absorbed in his computer work that he lost all connection with Rebecca. He recognized that this was one of the ways that his obsessive and rigid self-protections showed themselves. Rebecca acknowledged that her part of the conflict was comfortable to her. This caused her to make unilateral decisions about dinner.

Neither of us offered any unsolicited advice about what the other should do to repair or deal with our wounds. Neither made the other wrong or silly for being wounded. We both listened and appreciated the important and painful reasons each had for reacting in such self-protected ways. Because of this, we were able to reach a point in our discussion where there was no residue from the incident left in either of us. Instead, we had again started feeling nourished by and nourishing toward each other.

We then talked about how we would handle similar situations in the future until we knew what each of our new loving behaviors would be.

David agreed that he would find a way to work on the computer with full concentration while not abandoning his connection with Rebecca and with the necessities of everyday life (like preparing meals). He invited Rebecca to check with him periodically also, without fear of reprisal for disturbing him.

Rebecca agreed that she would interrupt David (gently) whenever she needed to reconnect with him. She acknowledged that there indeed *was* no way to figure out what foods David might like; that his food phobias were too random and unpredictable. Therefore, she agreed not to assume on David's behalf what he would or wouldn't like; if she had doubts she'd check with him.

We went on to have a lovely evening together, feeling our hearts were connected without reserve. This result was particularly important because this conflict over something that looked relatively minor on the surface could actually have led to a very serious rift between us. The argument over the meal tapped into very old but still very powerful experiences of ourselves as inadequate and wrong. Any one issue of this same, apparently trivial variety could have led us into a downword spiral of power struggles. Yet, our relationship continues to be intimate, harmonious, and free of resentment, rancour, and power struggles.

Here is a summary of the process we used in this example and the process we use in all such conflicts:

- We each recognize a conflict when we see one. We don't shove it under the rug believing that it shouldn't be such a big deal.
- Once we realize we are in our self-protective modes and are attacking each other, we separate and vent our anger on our own, not at each other. To vent anger at each other when we are being self-protective only leads to cruelty and deepened wounds.
- We take time apart in order to discharge our blaming feelings. We then re-center and engage in an inner exploration to discover what had come up in ourselves to lead to the conflict.
- We come back together, at a time when we are ready to do so, to gently let one another in on what each had discovered about ourselves and our own part in what happened between us.
- We each suggest and agree to the realistic yet effective loving behaviors that each of us would happily do in order not to lose our loving connection in similar situations in the future.
- We keep talking until we feel lovingly reconnected and there is no residue left from the incident for either of us.
- Finally, we follow through on our loving behaviors.

We have developed the following chart to illustrate these principles for seeing conflict through from start to finish in a way that can lead to deepened intimacy and *no left-over ill effects*. We have also developed an eight-step exercise to help you practice the honest communication that leads to deeper intimacy.

The Grudermeyer Flow Chart for
Intimacy Development & Conflict Resolution

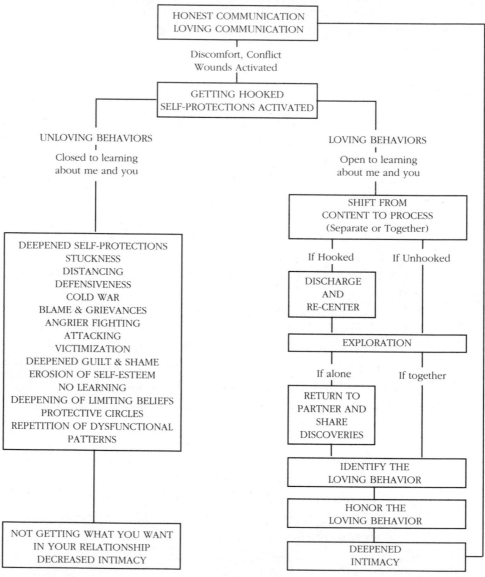

HONEST COMMUNICATION
LOVING COMMUNICATION

Discomfort, Conflict
Wounds Activated

GETTING HOOKED
SELF-PROTECTIONS ACTIVATED

UNLOVING BEHAVIORS

Closed to learning
about me and you

LOVING BEHAVIORS

Open to learning
about me and you

SHIFT FROM
CONTENT TO PROCESS
(Separate or Together)

If Hooked   If Unhooked

DEEPENED SELF-PROTECTIONS
STUCKNESS
DISTANCING
DEFENSIVENESS
COLD WAR
BLAME & GRIEVANCES
ANGRIER FIGHTING
ATTACKING
VICTIMIZATION
DEEPENED GUILT & SHAME
EROSION OF SELF-ESTEEM
NO LEARNING
DEEPENING OF LIMITING BELIEFS
PROTECTIVE CIRCLES
REPETITION OF DYSFUNCTIONAL
PATTERNS

DISCHARGE
AND
RE-CENTER

EXPLORATION

If alone   If together

RETURN TO
PARTNER AND
SHARE
DISCOVERIES

IDENTIFY THE
LOVING BEHAVIOR

HONOR THE
LOVING BEHAVIOR

NOT GETTING WHAT YOU WANT
IN YOUR RELATIONSHIP
DECREASED INTIMACY

DEEPENED
INTIMACY

Exercise 35A   The Grudermeyer Format for Conflict Resolution and Intimacy Renewal

This exercise is to be used when, during a conversation or other interaction, you and your partner begin to feel uncomfortable and disconnected. Each stage of the process is followed by questions that will be helpful to get you rolling and keep you focused on your part of the process.

Step 1.   Recognize that wounds are being hooked into and self-protections have been activated.

> Are my self-protections getting activated as we talk?

> What is the situation that is activating my self-protections?

Step 2.   Shift the focus from the conversation to the protections that have been activated.

> Am I willing to put aside my need to talk about the topic of conversation for a while so I can refocus my attention on exploring the emotions, wounds, or beliefs that are "up" in me right now?

> Am I willing to keep my feelings and pain company? (If I'm not willing, I will move into unloving behavior and all the toxic consequences that result.)

REBECCA:
> At this point, I often use the prayer, "Please help me be willing." It's a good prayer for when I'm too hooked to be willing by myself, yet I *want* to be willing.

Step 3.   Separate if necessary.

> Can I safely explore what is coming up within me in the presence of my partner or do I need to separate from him/her first?

> If I need to discharge some difficult feelings, is it both safe for me and okay with my partner if I do so in front of him/her? (If it's not okay, I still need to discharege first before I can continue to deal with our conflict, so we will need to separate for a while.)

Step 4.   Discharge and re-center.

What do I need to do to let go of my protections?

Am I acknowledging and releasing my protections instead of merely justifying them? (For further help with this, see "Summary: Ways to Move Out of Protections," page 115.)

Step 5.   Explore.

Now that I have moved out of blaming and self-protection, what are the emotions, old wounds, and beliefs that were triggered within me in this conflict?

Would it be better and safer for me and my partner if I did this exploration in front of my partner or by myself?

Have I continued to explore until I am clear about what came up within me during this conflict?

Am I focusing *solely* on clarifying my part in the problem? (Leave it up to your partner to focus on his/her part, in whatever way he/she wishes.)

I will know I have hit "paydirt" when I feel free of blaming my partner or feeling attacked by him/her.

Step 6.   Reconnect with your partner and share your discoveries.

If I have done my exploration apart from my partner, I will now let him/her know that I'm ready to reconnect and share what I have discovered about myself.

When my partner is also open to sharing what he/she has discovered, that is the time to sit down together and share both our discoveries.

Step 7.   Identify and honor the loving behavior.

What might help each of us respond more lovingly in similar situations in the future?

In what ways can my partner help me deal with my wounds?

In what ways can I help my partner deal with his/her wounds?

Once we have identified the loving behavior, we will agree to practice this loving behavior where possible, and we will follow through on the agreement.

Step 8.   Return to original conversation or interaction with deepened intimacy.

Is it important or relevant to return to the conversation or interaction we were having when the conflict first occurred?

If we do return to it, we will both be coming from a place of deepened openness and intimacy.

36. APPRECIATING YOUR LIFE

Appreciating both positive and negative experiences helps you to be at peace with whatever is in your life. A saying we've always liked is, "Life gives you two kinds of experiences—positive and negative. For those who learn only from their negative experiences, life offers only one kind of experience."

Most of us appreciate positive things—even though we sometimes fail to acknowledge it—but appreciating the opportunities given by the difficulties in our lives is a very different story. We tend to lapse into our protections rather than view our negative experiences as opportunities for learning.

Exercise 36A   Appreciating the Positive and the Negative

Part 1   Appreciating the "Positive" Experiences

Begin by thinking about those people who have helped you learn or supported you during your difficult times—the people who had faith in you. Among these special people may be relatives, spouses, teachers, or friends.

1.   Write your thoughts about the positive influence each one has had on your life.

2.   If possible, tell these people your feelings in person, on the phone, or in a letter.

3.   If you have difficulty in finding, feeling, and/or expressing your positive feelings, discover the self-limiting beliefs that are blocking you.

From Conflict to Caring

Part 2   Appreciating the "Negative" Experiences

This exercise is not just making lemonade out of lemons or looking for the silver lining. It is an opportunity to look deeply within and discover how and/or why you are not being loving to yourself or to another person. For example, being ill gives you the opportunity to look at your beliefs about how disease is contracted and cured; your feelings about being sick and needy; death (if it's a serious illness); your lifestyle, which may have contributed to your illness; and areas in which you may be emotionally stuck. Illness is not just about getting well again, it's about learning to create a healthier lifestyle.

The same is true for people in your life. People often complain that while one of their children is a delight, another one distresses them. That one is your teacher. Learning to love that child will be your best and most expanding lesson.

If you are married to someone who is so intelligent and powerful that you find yourself getting defensive or giving in, that is your opportunity to confront your insecurities and the beliefs that are causing them.

If you feel threatened or intimidated by someone, you have the opportunity to learn how to create peace instead of anxiety. With each person or situation, accept that he/she/it is a gift in your life to teach you something very important for your emotional and spiritual development. Ask yourself the following questions:

1.   Why am I reacting so intensely? What is the button being pushed? Who is this person reminding me of?

2.   What is my lesson here?

3.   What are the self-limiting beliefs that I need to correct?

Part 3   Appreciating the Everyday Problems

Just as you can learn from the major problems in your life, you can learn from the minor irritations: disappointments, unmet expectations, difficulties in your schedule, traffic jams, and so on. When faced with such annoyances, ask yourself the following questions:

1.   What is my spiritual lesson? What does this conflict have to teach me about letting go and having faith?

2. How can I turn this irritation into a positive experience, one that will allow me to feel peaceful and increase my self-esteem?

3. What self-limiting beliefs are getting in the way of that?

PRINCIPLES FOR RELATIONSHIPS

1. *My relationships are my opportunity to express myself as a loving person. How I express my love is a function of my own willingness to do so, not the result of how another person behaves.*

2. *Any difficult or painful moment in my relationships is a new opportunity for me to develop as a loving person. At the moment of conflict, I can choose to blame the other and the relationship, or, by my willingness to learn from the experience, I can use the occasion to expand my ability to love and to learn.*

3. *I am the one who generates my experience of my relationships through how I choose to act and react to whatever anyone does, and I am solely responsible for my feelings.*

4. *All my life's partners (mate, children, parents, friends) love me in their Higher Selves as I love them in my Higher Self. My partners are lovable in their Higher Selves as I am lovable in my Higher Self.*

5. *I can experience love and satisfaction whenever I choose. These feelings are possible at any time and place and in any circumstance, whenever I choose to be who I really am, my Higher Self.*

RECOMMENDED READING

Breaking Free from Compulsive Overeating by Geneen Roth (New York: MacMillan, 1984).

The Chalice and the Blade: Our History, Our Future by Riane Eisler (New York: Harper & Row, 1987).

Continuum Concept: Allowing Human Nature to Work Successfully by Jean Liedloff (Reading, Massachusetts: Addision-Wesley, 1977).

A Course in Miracles (The Foundation for Inner Peace, 1985).

For Your Own Good: Hidden Cruelty in Childrearing and the Roots of Violence by Alice Miller (New York: Farrar, Straus & Giroux, 1983).

Hearts that We Broke Long Ago by Merle Shain (New York: Bantam, 1985).

Love Is Letting Go of Fear by Gerald Jampolsky (Berkeley, California: Celestial Arts, 1979).

The Magic of Conflict: Turning a Life into a Work of Art by Thomas F. Crum (New York: Simon & Schuster, 1987).

Making Peace with Your Parents by Harold Bloomfield and Leonard Felder (New York: Ballantine, 1986).

Men Who Hate Women and the Women Who Love Them by Susan Forward (New York: Bantam, 1986).

One by Richard Bach (New York: William Morrow, 1988).

Open Mind, Open Heart: The Contemplative Dimension of the Gospel by Thomas Keating (Amity, New York: Amity House, 1986).

Out of the Shadows: Understanding Sexual Addiction by Patrick Carnes (Minneapolis: CompCare, 1983).

The Road Less Traveled by M. Scott Peck (New York: Simon & Schuster, 1980).

The Search for Existential Identity: Patient-Therapist Dialogues in Humanistic Psychology by James F.T. Bugental (San Francisco: Jossey-Bass, Inc., 1976).

Self-Parenting by John K. Pollard, III (Malibu, California: Generic Human Studies, 1987).

To Know as We Are Known: A Spirituality of Education by Parker Palmer (New York: Harper & Row, 1983).

When Society Becomes an Addict by Anne Wilson Schaef (New York: Harper & Row, 1988).

Women and Self-Esteem by Linda Tschirhart Sanford and Mary Ellen Donovan (New York: Penguin, 1985).

Women Who Love Too Much by Robin Norwood (Los Angeles: Jeremy Tarcher, 1985).

Your Erroneous Zones by Wayne Dyer (New York: Avon, 1977).